THE MOST SENSATIONAL LIFE STORY ---- SINCE THAT OF MALCOLM X!

Ibo

"Ibo" is available at your local bookstores. For special quantity discounts on bulk purchases for sales promotions, fund raising or educational use, write or telephone the Promotion Manager, Bethune Publishing Co., P.O. Box 14947, Detroit, Michigan 48214, 313-393-8926.

Ibo

The Untold Story Behind Mark Clyde Bethune/Ibo Omar

Winnifred Bethune-Griffin

Bethune Publishing • Detroit

If you purchase this book without a cover, you should be aware that this book is stolen property. It was reported as "unsold and destroyed" to the publisher and neither the author nor the publisher has received any payment for this "stripped book".

Grateful acknowledgment is made for permission to reprint the following photographs:

Photograph #4
Copyright© 1973 by The New Pittsburgh Courier

Photograph #5, #6
Copyright© 1973 by The Michigan Chronicle

Copyright© 1995 Winnifred Bethune-Griffin
Back cover photograph Copyright© 1971 by the Bethune Family c/o Cecile Bethune Varner

Published by Bethune Publishing Company
Library of Congress Catalog Card No.: 96-75548
ISBN: 0-9650550-0-0

All rights reserved, which includes the right to reproduce this book or portions thereof in any form whatsoever except as provided by the U.S. Copyright Law. For information address Bethune Publishing Co., P.O. Box 14947, Detroit, Michigan 48214.

Printed in the UNITED STATES OF AMERICA

DEDICATION

This book is dedicated to my beloved brothers who directly and indirectly extended their physical beings for the ongoing struggle of African Americans.

Ibo Omar
March 26, 1950 - February 27, 1973

Michael Curry Bethune
June 3, 1946 - November 29, 1977

ACKNOWLEDGEMENTS

I would like to acknowledge foremost "God", my higher power, for guiding me through this monumental task;

My family members, who individually played significant roles in the creation and development of the contents of this book; I love you all from the depths of my heart:

Maternal Grandfather, Walter J. Searcey (1885-1965)

Maternal Grandmother, Yetive Eulalia Gunnthier Searcey (1887-1990)

Father, George F. Bethune (1917-1981)

Mother, Eulalia Searcey Bethune

Maternal Aunt, Bessie Searcy Davis (1922-1994)

Fraternal Aunt, Queen E. Bethune

(Sisters and Brothers):

Yetive (Pig)

Cecile (Bunnie)

Julian (Buddy)

G. Harriet (Kitty)

Franklyn (Frankie)

Michael (Mike) (1946-1977)

Cornel (Corn)

Horace

Fredderick (Freddy)

My Daughter (Terri G.) - What would I have done without your thorough research;

My Niece (Shawn) - I couldn't have made it without your superb computer literacy and research;

My Grandson (Mark Anthony) - Your curiosity regarding Grandma writing a book about your great uncle gave me continuous inspiration;

My remaining nieces and nephews - for your admiration and belief in me;

My first cousins Toni, Tia, Mario and the remaining eight of you for always sticking with me;

My advisor and friend, Dr. John T. Dziuba, M.D. - thanks for your confidentiality, support, encouragement, and belief in my abilities;

And a special thanks with much gratitude to the late "Jim Ingram", literary giant and activist, for publicly sharing the true identity of my brother "Ibo" during the early 70's, when those that knew/befriended him, had not the courage or had simply betrayed him. Ibo's family shall be forever indebted to you.

Winnifred Bethune-Griffin

An Open Letter to My Brother

March 26, 1994

My Dearest Brother,

  I am certain that you have questioned the reason(s) why it has taken some 21 years to come forth publicly with the truth about you and your life while physically on this earth. Please forgive my gross negligence and ignorance for lack of honor and dedication to you for "giving" the greatest gift that the almighty could bestow upon any man/woman, "the breath of Life", which you gave willingly for the betterment of your family and your people.

  Today is a very special day, your birthday. I know that you have been celebrating your birthday on the 21st of March, yet while closely reviewing your birth record it clearly states date of birth, March 26, 1950. Please again forgive your family for gross negligence. Also, your birth record indicated your race as being "colored" which truly convinces me that you never had the original copy (smile).

  I would like to update you on a few significant events that have taken place over the past years: your brother Michael, departed this life November 29, 1977, the causative factor is pretty much what you would have expected; while engaged in the sales of "death heroin", he was shot several times in the midst of a robbery by his girlfriend's other lover, who had a two-fold motive: sick jealousy and entrapped by the mighty powers of "king heroin". Our father, so overwhelmed by the grief of Michael's death and yours, which he kept hidden, just gave up his will to live, of course with other physical complications January 10, 1981. Mama, as I am sure you expected, lived to the magnificent age of 103, remaining strong and beautiful as ever. Our mother is doing well and is quite elated over the writing of your life story.

As for myself, I have recently completed the most difficult and challenging process of transformation from Negro to African American with much dignity. To intiate this process, I utilized the twelve steps to combat the 24 hour challenge of my chemical dependency and from that point I was then able to challenge the process of acquiring my true nationality and identity.

Now my dear brother "Ibo", I have reached the level of emotional maturity with a sound mind and clear conscience to compose your life story with great honor. It is my greatest hope that through the almighty and the spirit of you that is lodged within my mind and heart, that I have successfully fulfilled the most important mission of my life.

                                              With Eternal Love,

                                              Sis

                                              Winnie

CONTENTS

1.	Ibo's Day	1
2.	Mission Accomplished	10
3.	526 E. Elizabeth	25
4.	Mark Clyde	37
5.	Ibo Omar	55
6.	The Hunt	82
7.	Awakening/Epilogue	112

Ibo

Ibo's Day

The preparation for Mark's/Ibo's final day physically upon this earth is recalled by the senior family members as being quite different from the typical burial preparation. Mark/Ibo was not just a biological son, brother, cousin, or close friend. He had become an extension of his people, "African American People", who possessed the right to be as equally involved in the preparation as did his biological family members. I am absolutely certain that Mark/Ibo would have had this no other way.

Bunnie recalls her greatest concern. How were we going to obtain Mark's/Ibo's body from Atlanta, Georgia and get through the legal red tape in view of the circumstances surrounding his death? She anxiously awaited the arrival of our mother, Kitty and Buddy, from New York State. When all of the senior family members were finally in Detroit they met at Aunt Bessie's house on LaSalle Blvd, which was the family headquarters. Also present were various members of the organization. Their interest and concern for Ibo and his commitment was far beyond our intellectual grasps at that time.

During the planning process, I remember my mother being rather quiet and solemn and having very little input. The unbearable pain and guilt she felt within was displayed about her entire face. What could I or anyone else say or do for her to ease the tremendous burden that was upon her. Unfortunately, this same burden is lodged within her heart and mind to this very day. Fortunately, she had her younger sister, aunt Bessie, whom she loved dearly, who stepped right in and did for her what she lacked the strength and will to do.

It was initially decided that Aunt Bessie would accompany our mother to Atlanta to secure Mark's/Ibo's body and that Stinson Funeral Home on West Grand Boulevard would handle the funeral arrangements. It was requested by the organization that the final ceremony be held at the Shrine Of The Black Madonna with the family consenting to their request. The next day we met with the funeral director at Stinson and shared with him our plans for securing Mark's/Ibo's body. He at that time informed the family that Stinson had a private plane and could eliminate the added stress upon us by transporting the body via their plane. For this we were very grateful. When Mr. Stinson got to Atlanta, Georgia, the red tape awaited him as we had anticipated. Eventually the Atlanta Police Department released the body.

When Stinson called informing us that Mark's/Ibo's body had arrived we all anxiously, yet reluctantly rushed to the funeral home to assess its condition. Prior to letting anyone view the body, the funeral director explicitly informed each family member that Mark/Ibo had not taken his own life. Kitty asked the funeral director if there was any disfigurement about the face and head that would prevent the body from being shown. The funeral director replied that this was what he was about to explain - If Mark had shot himself in the head as the media had stated and the death certificate stated there would surely have been much disfigurement, yet in Mark's case there was none. He further concluded that he had prepared enough bodies in his career to know the damage any caliber of bullet could/would do to any part of the body.

Bunnie vividly recalls the bullet mark on Mark's/Ibo's forehead being approxiamtely the size of the tip of a small female baby finger with his face and head in tact. Further, that he looked like his usual self and had a healthy appearance as though he had taken adequate care of himself with no signs of dissipation. "In no way, she said, did Mark look as though he had reached the point of suicide, instead he had a total look of fullfillment." Who could know him any better than Bunnie for she had been like his mother since birth and for that matter a mother to all of us. My greatest concern when assessing his body was making sure that it was "Mark/Ibo". As Buddy, Frankie, Michael, Cornel, and I viewed his body together, we examined it from head to toe. I remember touching the so called suicide bullet wound to his head which was so small you had to really look close to see it. The thought never entered my mind that my brother had taken his own life. He simply had no reason to. He was a winner. He would never give up. As I touched and looked at the extent of the black surgical thread about his chest area I thought, did they have to cut him like this to see where the bullet went in his chest? Oh, how bitter I was about this. Then I felt the black braid on his wrist and I truly knew that was Ibo, for that braid was symbolic of his total identity - all that he believed in, all that he lived and died for. Somehow, some way, I wanted desperately to communicate with my bother as I intensely stared at his physical remains. There were numerous questions I needed answered, uncertainties that needed to be resolved. I longed for one of his secure hugs of reassurance.

I was so relieved that the senior family members had the responsibility of making the funeral arrangements because I wanted no parts of it. How could I take part in the funeral preparations for my brother whom I felt was still very much alive? I did not understand my feelings/belief at that time. Yet I did know that there was something very, very mystical about everything involving Mark/Ibo.

In view of the intense issues involving Mark's/Ibo's death, it was suggested by the funeral director that the funeral be held at Stinson instead of at the Shrine of the Black Madonna as originally planned. The senior family members agreed especially due to the family being concerned about things getting out of control. The organization wasn't too pleased about this. However, they were cooperative and supportive of the family's decision. After having made the final arrangements that day, Bunnie recalls having the most radiant feeling when she arrived home and found friends awaiting her as far back as early childhood and friends of friends. They were all extending well wishes and support on behalf of her brother's most courageous mission for the struggle of black people. "This support, she said, reinforced what she knew her brother fought and died for, the awakening and positive networking among black people as a whole in the development of productive living for all." She further recalls sharing with her friends that to some point she felt relieved. Her brother was no longer being pursued as the "mad dog killer" he had been so maliciously labeled. Hopefully one day the truth about his mission would surface.

The following day Mark's/Ibo's body was ready for public viewing. When the family arrived at Stinson's, the chapel had to be cleared for private family viewing. Before my very eyes were hundreds of black people waiting patiently in lines stretched up and down West Grand Boulevard and W. Warren avenue, to view the physical remains of "my" brother. As I walked up and down these lines greeting and conversing with the majority of these people I did not know, I concluded, that Mark/Ibo had become one of their leaders. They had experienced a revelation in the giving of his life, that I as his blood sister had yet to experience. Each day that Mark's/Ibo's body laid in state, the people stood in these extensive lines to see him from the time the funeral home opened to the very minute it closed. His body was guarded 24 hours by the organization with the same quality of reverance as our profound leader "Malcolm X".

Masses of people gathered at and outside of Aunt Bessie's house the night of the wake. Kitty recalls never experiencing anything like this in her life. She truly did not understand the Black Movement at that time, feeling rather uneasy and somewhat frightened. She could not understand why the organization had taken such an active role with his funeral proceedings as though they were family members. "Such audacity", she thought. In her own words she felt as though the family had been robbed of Mark, now belonging to the people who placed him at such high esteem. She resented the fact that the people knew him much better than she, his own sister. This wake was not like the traditional wakes I had attended with the reminiscing about the deceased and lots of spirits to ease the pain of the loss. Instead, it was like a formal gathering with endless individual group discussions and testimonials regarding the very essence of the 86 day manhunt. Two issues that were made clear among this mass of black people was that they knew Mark/Ibo had not taken his own life and that his mission was for the "betterment" of his people for which he gave his own life.

It was March 3, 1973, approximately 12:15 p.m. and I with my family had arrived at Stinson's Funeral Home on West Grand Boulevard in Detroit for the exit ceremony from this earth of Mark/Ibo. When I stepped from the family car, there were hundreds of black people with the vast majority standing on the outside of this modest funeral home to acknowledge this special day of my brother's. The last time I had witnessed masses of black folks coming together in such a meaningful manner in Detroit, was in 1963 when our magnificent leader, Dr. Martin Luther King, Jr. spoke at Cobo Hall. I cannot convey in words the magnititude of the sensation that filled my heart to be amidst multitudes of "my people" who had come to honor "my blood brother".

Again the chapel had to be cleared out so that the traditional family could be seated, yet we realized that all black people were a part of his family as well. Bunnie vividly recalls the physical appearance of the chapel as being one of the most beautiful sights she had ever seen. Flowers dominated the room from every angle, from organizations, businesses, sororities, families, individuals. There were dozens and dozens of red roses with black and green ribbons stating "we love you". "God and peace be with you." Present were black people from every walk and way of life, ranging from dignitaries to the very poor. The atmosphere amongst the people was very serious, orderly, quiet, still and sad. You could feel the love, compassion, and respect within your soul. It was like a sudden magnetic kinship. Was this the coming together of black people that Mark/Ibo had often spoke about?

The eulogy was delivered by Chokwee Lumumba, an official of the Republic of New Africa. An article from the Michigan Chronicle, March 10, 1973, **"Mark Bethune - Jekyle or Hyde**, well summarizes its contents:

The eulogy from Chokwee Lumumba, an official of The Republic of New Africa, attested to what many of his friends said about Mark Bethune - that he was extremely concerned about the plight of the black community, but more worried about the future of black children and was angry over the spreading narcotics traffic.

"He accepted the fact that he would accelerate the time

he had to die", Lumumba said. "We must demonstrate the fact that we understand what Bethune was about...In the final analysis, the source of the supply of narcotics must be cut off. The reason Bethune is lying in that casket, he said, is because people in the community have not attempted to deal with the problem. You are going to have to move against the dope man or live in constant terror."

Attorney Kenneth Cockrel also talked about getting rid of the drug menance, or live in constant terror. "You ain't heard none of those big-time leaders say anything about what Boyd, and Bethune were about. From this day on, we can build a level of consciousness inside this community, and we can say they have not died in vain", he said. "We can say that John Percy Boyd did not die in vain and Mark Bethune did not die in vain, and Hayward Brown will not rot inside a prison."

One young sister, whose name we did not get, was almost overwhelmed with emotions as she said, "He (Bethune) wanted to save the children. He wanted to save the babies. He put his life on the line for black people because he couldn't stand what was happening. He got out there by himself because he had to." And she broke in sobs.

The speakers and testimonials proceeded to go on. The funeral director unwillingly had to discontinue them for the sake of time. I am certain that these testimonials, if allowed, would have continued throughout the day. As we left the chapel to convey Mark/Ibo to his final resting place, there were cars already lined up for miles to accompany us to that destination - Detroit Memorial Park Cemetary on 13 Mile in Warren, Michigan. Those that weren't in cars stood reverently in the cold, sobbing, some in dismay, trying to get a glimpse of the casket or touch it, if they could. It was drapped with the black, green and red liberation flag, symbolic of "our" African heritage, our land, and the endless blood we had and would continue to shed. The warmth that I felt from the presence and unity of all these black people, "my people", I shall always cherish.

The City of Detroit did not provide us with police escorts to Detroit Memorial Park, as is the case with large and dignitary funerals, for obvious reasons. Instead, Buddy, along with a few close friends from New York City, assumed the responsibility of directing this massive funeral procession. Might I add that they did a magnificent job, with not an accident occurring.

As we arrived at the cemetary, officials awaited to greet the family and to instruct the remaining hundreds of people to park their cars by encircling the cemetary. The burial ceremony did not take place until each and every car was parked and all were gathered as best they could at the burial site. The ceremony was brief, ending quietly and peacefully. Well wisheres took pieces of flowers as memorabilias as they wept and embraced. There was no doubt that Ibo had extended himself to his people. They were now extending their gratitude, love and loyalty to him. This day, without question was, "Ibo's Day".

Mission Accomplished

It was Thanksgiving Day, 1972, and as with most Thanksgivings, my immediate family was gathered in Detroit at the home of our second eldest sister "Bunnie" whom we all praised and believed could prepare a meal better than anyone on earth. My oldest brother Buddy came from New York City to join us, upon Mark's insistance. As always anticipated, his very presence meant laughter, partying, and lots of fun, fun, fun.

In the midst of the feasting, laughter and fun, Mark asked me to take a ride with him in his usual "directive" manner. I obliged, not really having much of a choice. I could sense that "Little-Big" Brother was in one of his intense serious moods and had something important to do. As we were riding, Mark began to tell me that the time had come - my response was - "the time had come for what?" His reply was - "you all have just not been taking me seriously - I have been talking about my purpose and mission for a long time." He proceeded to talk about the destruction of Black Americans through genocide, utilizing strategic devices such as: drugs (specifying heroin and alcohol), birth control devices (specifying birth control pills), young black male homicide via drug wars, Local Police Department (S.T.R.E.S.S.), Vietnam

11   Ibo

War - poverty, illiteracy and the list went on. "My mission is to stop the destruction of my people. "To begin with, heroin must no longer be available for use - Therefore, the source "must be eliminated" - This is where I will start." I then asked, "just how do you plan to do all of this, especially eliminating "heroin"." His reply was, "Little Sis, be quiet, don't ask anymore questions and just listen - further, you know I continue to remind you that Black Sisters must learn to listen and refrain from asking so many questions and let the Black Brother take charge of things." Though I was three years his senior, I obediently followed through with his instructions.

"Now listen closely", he said. "I want you to tell our mother that if she doesn't see me again I am o.k. and not to worry - if she does see me again I will be in a "casket". "He hugged and kissed me, told me he loved me and not to worry. As we rode back to my sister's home, there was absolute silence. I told him to be careful and got out of the car. He waved and drove off. Of course I didn't take him seriously. In fact, as he himself said, none of us ever did. I, at that time 25 years old, had very little interest in Black Power, the Movement/Struggle - loved drinking alcohol/taking uppers, partying and could see no detriment it had upon Black People as a whole during that period of time. However, I was against the Vietnam War because it was taking many young, black, male lives. Heroin, I thought was the "demon" of all drugs, and was in agreement that it totally needed to be eliminated from the streets of Detroit especially. I didn't know how on earth

Mark was going to eliminate it.

Again - I thought about the last thing Mark told me - "I want you to tell our mother if she doesn't see me ever again, I am o.k. and not to worry - if she does, I will be in a "casket", and again and again.

<u>Toledo, Ohio</u>

It is February 27, 1973. My only child/daughter, Terri, is residing with her father and his second wife for the remainder of the school year. Terri is six years of age. The family is gathered around the T.V. watching the National News, which was a daily ritual for that household. All eyes are focused on a body being lowered from the dormitory roof of Morris-Brown College in Atlanta, Georgia. The cover that conceals the body is not tucked securely and the victim's head drops to the side vividly exposing the face. Terri anxiously rushes to the T.V. screen pointing and screaming, "Daddy, Daddy, that's my Uncle Mark. Her father replies, "No, baby, that's not your Uncle Mark. Terri insists, "Yes it is Daddy", "See", as she slides her finger across the name on the screen - "MARK BETHUNE".

<u>Detroit, February 27, 1973</u>

That day the sky was as clear blue as the ocean and the sun was shining so brightly it blinded you. The air was cold and crisp. It was such a beautiful, beautiful pre-Spring day. I shall never forget it because it was the day prior to my mother's birthday, February 28. Riding in a cab on my way home with some friends, the cab driver abruptly blurted out as he turned the volume up on his radio, "They have caught that other guy in Atlanta too. What's his name - Bethune, yeah, Bethune, and he's been shot. I think he's dead." "You don't know what the hell you're talking about. John Percy Boyd was shot and killed in Atlanta the other day, that's what they're talking about," I said. His reply was, "No sister", "Can't you hear?" "Mark Bethune has been shot and they think he's dead." My friend then stated, "Mark Bethune is her blood brother, man." The cab driver replied, "Sweetheart, I am so sorry." My chest felt as though a ton of bricks had fallen on it. Immediately I asked the cab driver to stop at the liquor store - I needed something instantly to deal with this. The best friend I knew at that time - alcohol. After having drank several gulps of Barcardi's Dark rum and coke I could feel my heart beating fast, experiencing a sense of helplessness, confusion, anger, pain and fear. From that point I could think of no where to escape but to my Aunt's for comfort and to try to sort things out. As I exited the cab somewhat hesistant to enter my aunt's home, I could sense the tension, pain, outbursts, and remorse that awaited me. For this was the family home, large enough to accomodate myself - 10 brothers and sisters, my 11 first cousins, senior family members and numerous friends at any given time. It was a place of reference for the entire family, especially for Mark who spent many of his teen and young adult years preaching the message for those who desired and "did not" desire to listen.

They expected me. Aunt Bessie was crying intensely,

my cousins were crying, shouting, wanting revenge. Yet one thing puzzled us - why and how did Mark end up in Atlanta. It remains a mystery to this very date.

There was one thing that was truly a reality that day; Mark's physical departure from Earth. The media must have aired my brother's body being lowered from the dormitory roof with his head dropping to the side vividly displaying his face on an hourly basis. It was as though they had to convey to the entire country that Mark Clyde Bethune was truly dead. The experience of viewing my brother's remains repeatedly in this manner and the eerie moans of the crowd at the actual site was similar to the experience I had at age eight; having opened up the Jet Magazine to the centerfold and traumatized by the face of Emmett Till. As I further recall his mother stated beside the picture "I want the whole world to see what they have done to my son". I shall never forget that experience for I had nightmares for many years following. Just as I shall never forget how I was repeatedly compelled to initially view my brother's remains, with his head dropping from beneath a cloth covered slack as his body was lowered from the dormitory roof of Morris Brown College. Each time this surfaces into my memory it feels as though I physically have a stone lodged in the center of my heart.

As the day progressed my gulping of alcohol increased. For some odd reason, my Number 1 coping companion just wasn't working. My objective was to pass out and deal with this monumental event at some other time. Well it simply didn't happen. I became so overwhelmed from conversing with friends and persons I didn't even know, seeking answers to the "how's" and "why's" that I could not provide and would have not provided had I known.

At some point I realized that I hadn't conversed with my mother and father or brothers and sisters. Mama (my Grandmother) of course in view of her great fortitude and independence had taken a bus from her senior housing complex downtown to my Aunt's home on the west side. I recall her walking around calmly, yet in rigid manner, telling everyone "it's going to be alright, it's going to be alright". The American Indian blood that flowed through her veins was so profound at that time that her round face, distinct high cheekbones, high-bridged nose, displayed no inner emotion.

Where was Michael, I thought? He was my only brother living in Detroit who unfortunately had a serious heroin addiction and I was praying he hadn't over indulged. Well eventually he made it to our Aunt's home, cool and reserved, trying hard not to show his inner feelings, voicing his favorite line - "Well, you know you must take the bitter with the sweet". I then called my oldest sister Yetive to see how she was feeling. Her voice displayed some anxiousness. She assured me that Mark was o.k. now and that we all had to stay calm and in control. While talking with my second oldest sister Bunnie, I could tell she had been crying. Her voice was rather chokey as she spoke, saying "well Winnie, I'm just glad this is all over, it has taken such a toll on me". This is the sister that had fed him his bottles, changed his diapers, was a mother to him, needless to say to all her younger brothers and sisters. Yes, I truly understood the burden that was lifted from her heart. Calling my father, I truly dreaded because we were just beginning to re-unite with him, in addition to his poor mental and physical status. As anticipated he was rather reserved acknowledging that he was aware of Mark's death. I could sense he was fighting hard not to show his emotions. I wonder just what he felt inside now having lost his youngest child and son in such a tragic manner. My brother Frankie was residing in Ann Arbor, attending the University of Michigan. I was sure he was aware of the terrifying day's events and would be contacting the family soon. When I did talk with him he shared that he had been drinking throughout the day, trying to make sense of this madness and how awfully bitter, angry, and hurt he felt. Buddy, my oldest brother, who lived in Bronx, New York, didn't appear too shaken. He vowed that he would be handling all matters pertaining to Mark's death.

<u>Rochester, New York - February 27,1973</u>

Remembering what Mark had requested that I convey to our Mother the last day I saw and talked to him, I somewhat regretted that I hadn't. My mother lived in Rochester, New York along with my brother Cornel and youngest brothers Freddy and Horace. Kitty, my third oldest sister also lived in Rochester, New York with her family. As had expected, Cornel was taking Mark's death with immense pain and bitterness.

They were extremely close. Freddy was very angry and bitter. Horace was very remorseful and sad. I recall Kitty sharing that all of this seemed so unreal. It was as though she was in a state of shock. My mother was rather quiet with very little to say, quite unlike herself during those years. I repeated to her what Mark had requested - "Tell our mother if she doesn't see me again I am o.k. - if she does, I will be in a casket". Of course her response was why hadn't I told her? My reply was, "I really didn't believe him or maybe I just didn't want to believe him".

The Detroit News, Feruary 28, 1973

$9,000 REWARD FOR BETHUNE - TIPSTER URGED

Full payment of "secret service reward totaling $9,000.00 in the Mark C. Bethune manhunt will be recommended by Martin S. Hayden, Editor of the Detroit News.

Bethune, 22, badly wounded by a shot from a policeman's 45 caliber pistol died by his own hand yesterday afternoon when trapped on the rooftop of a downtown Atlanta college dormitory.

Shot in the chest and with police closing in on him, Bethune put his .357 magnum pistol to his head and pulled the trigger, ending his life.

Thus ended one of the biggest manhunts in recent Detroit history - one that reached to Atlanta - for the three men sought in the shootings of five Detroit S.T.R.E.S.S. officers in December and the killing of a sixth.

Hayden said today he will recommend to a special citizen's review committee that the rewards be paid to an

Mission Accomplished   18

anonymous Atlanta man who tipped police to Bethune's whereabouts in the dormitory.

The tipster had stopped Lt. D.E. (Ike) Brown on an Atlanta street and asked if he would be rewarded through the Detroit News Secret Witness Plan - that he had read about in the two Atlanta newspapers. Assured by the officer that he would be eligible, the informant said that Bethune had been hiding in the dormitory of Morris-Brown College, an all black institution. This information led to the police chase that ended in Bethune's self-inflicted death.

An Atlanta policeman on the campus, Horace Walker, Jr., ordinarily a traffic patrolman, fired the shot that hit Bethune in the chest. Walker at first said he had side-stepped a shot that he thought Bethune had fired. It was later ascertained, however, that Bethune had not fired at Walker because the fugitive's pistol had been fired only once - the bullet he put in his own head.

Although Walker's bullet might well have proved fatal, it did not kill Bethune. The Detroiter, realizing he was incapacitated and trapped, ended his own life by shooting himself in the head, according to Atlanta authorities. No one knew that at that time, it was only established later by an autopsy and ballistic test.

"As I got there, I heard a noise on the roof," Walker said. "I thought that might be Bethune, so I leaned out where I could see up at him. He spotted me and took aim. I jumped sideways as he fired. I don't know where his bullet hit. He started back towards the open window he had emerged from; I took aim and when he turned to fire a second shot, I beat him to it. He went down and out of sight."

The other officers, not sure that Bethune was dead, kept their guns aimed on his fallen form from windows, but did not go onto the roof until a helicopter had landed other officers there. The officer who first turned Bethune over said he was breathing, but died soon afterwards.

The Detroit News - February 28, 1973
DETROIT'S DEADLIEST MANHUNT

Mark Clyde Bethune's self-inflicted fatal gunshot wound on an Atlanta rooftop yesterday put an end to the most intensive and deadly manhunt in Detroit's history. A trail of violence which started with a gunfight December 4th on a street corner a block from the University of Detroit left five men dead and at least seven persons wounded or hurt. It disrupted the lives of hundreds perhaps thousands of persons.

The 86-day manhunt for Bethune, 22, and his two companions, John Percy Boyd, 23, and Hayward Brown, 18, was concentrated in the Detroit area. But before it ended, the search had spread over large areas of the United States and Canada.

Today Brown, captured Jan 12, and now awaiting trial for murder, assault, and arson is the only one of the trio alive. Boyd was slain Friday when he tried to shoot it out with an Atlanta policeman.

It all began with a stake out by a crew of S.T.R.E.S.S. - Stop The Robberies Enjoy Safe Streets - officers Dec 4 near a suspected dope pad on Stoepel in the Livernois-McNichols area of Northwest Detroit.

On Jan. 11, Wayne Circuit Judge Thomas J. Foley ordered police to refrain from harassing relatives and friends of the fugitive trio. He threatened to jail any officers who violated the order.

On Jan. 12, the elusive trio surfaced again. This time in a bizarre firebombing of the Planned Parenthood Office on the Second Floor of the Medical Plaza Building near Wayne State University. Two women were injured - one, a doctor, by jumping out of a window.

Brown, carrying two loaded pistols, was captured after a chase and struggle. Police said he told them that the firebombing was intended to create a situation like that in New Orleans where a sniper killed six persons and wounded 16 from a downtown hotel roof before he was killed himself. Though Brown was captured, Boyd and Bethune could not be found following the firebombing. On the same day, the Detroit City Council held a hearing on charges of police brutality and harrassment in connection with the manhunt.

It was a bullet from a .357 magnum which Bethune fired into his own head yesterday after he had been wounded by police, bringing the terrifying odyssey of the three young Detroit gunmen to an end.

But the repercussions may be felt for a long time. Brown's chief attorney, Kenneth Cockrel, has already indicated that he will plead self defense for his client and that he will use the trial for a renewed assault on the whole concept behind the already controversial STRESS effort.

21   Ibo

The Detroit News, February 28, 1973

ELDER BETHUNE HAS NO GRUDGE

"I don't blame Atlanta or Detroit police for the death of my son. I blame the environment in which he had to grow up". A soft spoken George Bethune, 56, made that statement yesterday in reaction to the death of his son, Mark Clyde Bethune.

The elder Bethune yesterday sat quietly in the living room of his east side home and tried to explain "how my son went wrong" but said he had not seen the boy for a year.

He said he and his wife were divorced in 1958 and that his wife obtained custody of the children and placed them in a boarding home on Detroit's "west side".

The father said he did not know where his son had been living but he thought it was somewhere in Detroit.

"I thought he was attending Wayne State University but I found out from my daughter that he had joined some type of Black Revolutionary Movement", the elder Bethune said. "She told me he got into a bad group at WSU, and also said he appeared to have been using drugs and carried several guns on him. The next time I heard about Mark he was in New York with his mother." The elder Bethune continued, "I understood he came back to Detroit last summer". Bethune said he found it difficult to believe that his son could kill anyone. "I don't believe he could; when he was young he was timid. Still, because he was in that Movement, I can't say what his motives were or what motivated him." "Things went well for our family until I had a semi-stroke in 1952. I was working and we had a little money. We were happy and content."

The Detroit News, March 1, 1973

THE MYSTERY OF BOYD, BETHUNE, AND BROWN

Bethune meanwhile, came to Detroit in his late teens from Rochester, New York. He attended both Northern and Central High Schools, where officials said he had "serious academic difficulties". One of four brothers and three sisters, Bethune was reported by police to have been admitted for mental observation at Wayne County General Hospital, although friends dispute this. Regardless, Bethune was enrolled at Wayne State University as a Liberal Arts student in the Fall of 1969 through a federally funded program for under-achievers.

It was at Wayne State that Bethune discovered Political Activism. He took to wearing a single gold earring and began talking about "social revolution", friends say.

Several persons remember him at various meetings in the University's Student center, where he espoused a variety of radical causes. At one informal student gathering, he is said to have exhibited a sign urging revolutionaries to "kill a pig".

Dr. David Kidd, a Methodist Minister who is a Chaplain at the school's Religious Center, remembers him as "very bright". "He used to stop by and visit occasionally", Dr. Kidd said. "I always rather liked him; he had a good head on his shoulders."

In January 1971, Bethune dropped out of Wayne. He traveled to Atlanta, where he joined the Black Panther Party.

Later, he moved to Los Angeles, where he picked up some identification which listed his name as "Marcus Jones".

He returned to Detroit in early 1972. While not enrolled at Wayne, he continued to hang around its Student Union. He rented an apartment in Highland Park.

THE CONFLICT over the motives which led the trio to become the most hunted men in Detroit history began last Fall. It involves drugs and two sharply different views as to why the three became mixed up with the dealers.

Detroit police say the three were hired as "shot guns" or guards for a major narcotic dealer on the west side. Their job, police claimed, was to protect drug couriers on their rounds of area dope dens.

Police suggest that in late November Boyd and Bethune recieved a sort of underworld promotion. They supposedly were given a "contract" or an order to kill a Highland Park narcotics dealer. On November 29 the two were accused of killing one man and wounding another in Bethune's apartment. They were identified from police mug shots but never apprehended. On December 27, the three alledgely had another run-in with the law. This time they were accused of killing one officer and seriously wounding another who attempted to question them as they left a west side house that had been under police surveillance.

At one point, police hinted that the drug dealers were also after the three because the heat was too much. They said they had evidence that the men turned on the dealers and were robbing dope dens.

Evidence now indicates that the Highland Park killing was not the result of an underworld contract, but merely the result of a robbery that went too far. The two that were shot had no ties with drug trafficking, police later learned.

Still another version of the story says that Boyd and Bethune thought they had abducted drug dealers and they were trying to get the names of their supplier.

Police have been told by many sources that none of the three men used drugs. Police found a quantity of anti-drug information and posters in Bethune's apartment.

No trace of narcotics and no evidence of needle marks were found in the autopsy on Boyd and Bethune's bodies in Atlanta.

Relatives and close friends of all deny their involvement in drugs and say the men were trying to get pushers out of the Black Community.

Others have speculated that it was their hatred of drugs which got them into this in the first place. Adding further to the confusion is Bethune's father, George, a 56 year old disabled veteran. The elder Bethune said "he understood his son did use drugs and carried several guns."

Two days after the manhunt violence in Atlanta, authorities still are unable to determine the motives behind the bloody shootings.

What was it that caused three Detroiters to be the city's most sought after fugitives?

The answer may never be known.

526 E. Elizabeth

Perhaps the most significant event for Mark occurred during his first two years of life, having all began at 526 E. Elizabeth Street, Detroit, Michigan, early 1950's. 526 E. Elizabeth was a large brick two family flat which sat in back of the noted Stroh's Brewery. This two family structure was the home for my family and four additional families. During this time period, African American families consisting of a large number of offsprings found it extremely difficult to find housing. They were often compelled to rent rooms within single housing complexes. This was primarily the only manner in which shelter was available to non-home owners. Further, owners providing shelter for these families on a rental basis took in consideration the number of offsprings, setting additional costs to the base rent per child. My mother recalls our rent being over $200.00 for two rooms.

My family, consisting of my parents, seven brothers and sisters and one on the way occupied one bedroom and the dining room of the upper flat; excluding my oldest sister Yetive, who lived with my grandparents since birth.

The second family consisted of a husband, wife, and three children, whose primary rental space was a large bedroom. The owner occupied a large and small adjoining room of the same upper flat which my sister Kitty recalls had lavish furnishings. The remaining bedroom was occupied by a single woman. Residing in the lower flat was the owner's sister-in-law and her three children.

The imposed living arrangements for all of these families was similar to communal living. Aside from each family's identified rental quarters, "all" utilized the bathroom, kitchen and living room equally, well, as equally as conditions permitted. During this period, this was the non-blood related extended African American family that society tended not to expound too heavily upon in their eloquent studies of urban industrial living for obvious reasons; which is quite similar if not identical to the same living conditions of today that urban African Americans are subjected to in view of their socio/environmental, economical and personal deprivations.

Every adult within this living confine realized that though the quarters were close, allowing very little space for individual family independence, this was home for the time being. It was necessary to develop genuine respect, concern, support and love for each other to maintain survival.

It is year 1950 and my mother is pregnant with Mark. She recalls her pregnancy as being relatively happy and stable. My father, a tailor, and might I add a very fine tailor, was attending upholstering school to enhance his marketable skills. Bunnie recalls him studying diligently at night and my mother being so proud of him, always boasting about his superior intelligence. He loved sewing dearly and was always making clothing for our mother and his children. For the special occasion of Mark's birth he designed a floor length house coat for our mother to wear upon her arrival from the hospital. This garment was made of ticking cloth with a pink/white floral and stripe pattern, double breasted with a wide shawl-like collar. Although Kitty was only 9 years old, she recalls this garment so distinctly because of how pretty our mother looked in it. With the remainder of the material he creatively designed a mattress for Mark's crib and a pleated bumper pad. Everyone in the house boasted about how adorable the finishing touches made the crib stand out from typical cribs.

The day Mark was brought home from the hospital was indeed an especially happy time for us, as had been with all new additions to the family. As with tradition, there was a grand celebration with lots of food and spirits. All of the children were so happy and proud of their new little brother who definitely had the distinct profile of a Bethune; big head, huge brown eyes and golden brown skin. He, from all aspects as the old folks say was a fine, healthy and strong man-child.

Kitty, who was always close to our mother, was just fascinated by Little Mark as she recalls. On one occasion while he was being diapered and all powdered-up, Kitty anxiously asked our mother if she could hold him for a little while. Our mother's response was no, because he was too heavy and she might drop him. So she just patiently waited until our mother left out of the room momentarily and quickly picked

Mark up, almost dropping him as she was startled by his huge brown eyes.

Because Mark was such a good baby and hardly ever cried, he was taken to church almost every Sunday with the rest of the children. We attended St. Matthew Episcopal Church, which was directly up the street from where we lived. Mark was also christened at this parish. Ironically, he was named by my mother after the Episcopal school and church she attended from childhood to graduation, St. Mark's in Birmingham, Alabama. His middle name was taken from the priest of the parish, Father Clyde Perry.

During Mark's first six months of growth it was detected that he wasn't a very happy baby, for his eyes were rather sad and droopy and he rarely smiled. He certainly had loads of attention, especially from his numerous brothers and sisters who loved him dearly. I guess it was his unique little personality in the stages of development.

We remained on Elizabeth Street for approximately six months. Unfortunately, the owner decided to put her home up for sale, which meant our extended family we had grown to respect, love and trust had to search for housing. Everyone was extremely sad, yet what had to be done, had to be done.

Our mother was able to find an apartment building on Hendrie Street, yet the landlord specifically mandated that only three children would be allowed for a two bedroom apartment. Realizing the necessity of securing immediate housing for her family, she lied and assured the owner that she and her husband only had three children. Our father did not accompany her during this transaction because he always had problems coping in stressful situations; leaving such matters "always" for our mother to take care of. It came to her mind instantly that all her children, in excess of three, simply had to be hidden. How that would be accomplished on a day to day basis, she just couldn't worry about at the time. She was so grateful that she had found an apartment that was willing to take children.

In view of the rigorous job awaiting of keeping four of the children hidden to maintain shelter for us, it was decided that it would be less stressful for our mother to let Mark stay with our grandparents until suitable housing could be secured. Although the older children knew that this was temporary for the baby, they were deeply saddened by this. He was the baby and they just couldn't understand why he was chosen to live with Mama and Daddy (our grandparents). They lived way on the west side, which meant we wouldn't see him very often. Well this was something we had no control over at least for the time being.

In addition to the other dilemas we were forced to deal with, our family was not very financially stable during this period. Our father was not working very steadily and money was real tight. At one point the older children were taken out of school because there were no monies for clothing. All of the older children were very bright and did exceptionally well in their academic studies. Not being able to go to school was quite disheartening to them. Our mother being the proud and vain woman she was, refused to let her children be seen ragged in the public eye. With great determination she was able to obtain help through the Department of Social Services and got adequate clothing for all of us. This meant the older children could return to school and what a joyful occasion that was.

One day the landlord came over to pick up the rent and Michael, almost 5 years old with his usual rambunctious self, opened the door to greet the gentleman. The landlord had never seen him before and asked who he was; in the process of telling him he boasted about all his other brothers and sisters who lived there. When my mother came to the living room the landlord immediately confronted her regarding how many children she had. Of course she insisted that Michael was just fantisizing as most children do. The landlord replied, "Children never lie." At that point she apologized for being dishonest for obvious reasons. Through compassion, he understood, yet informed her that the rent would be raised somewhat. Of course this added more stress as we were already in a state of financial dilema, yet it brought much relief that she didn't have to hide her children anymore.

Since our family secret had surfaced to the landlord, Little Mark came home with the rest of his family. What a happy day that was. He had really grown in six months; trying to walk, saying simple words, and his head and eyes had gotten even bigger. His shy, withdrawn mannerism was more evident now that he was older, yet you could sense that he was happy to be home. Bunnie recalls how she kissed and hugged the little guy so, praying that he would never have to leave us again.

Mark's coming home certainly lifted the family's spirits. The older children were going to school regularly, and our father continued to work, perhaps not as much as he could have, yet it seemed as if things were going to be alright. Again we had established wholesome relationships with families in the apartment complex and on our street. It was the kind of supportive wholesome relationship that is the absent link within African American communities of today.

Our mother, over time, began to lose her resilience, experiencing periods of mild to severe depression. She believed that our family deserved a better status within this society, simply desiring the American Dream. It was extremely difficult for her to understand why our father, such a brilliant man, having graduated from Parker High School in Birmingham, Alabama with a 4.0 grade point average with perfect attendance throughout his 12 years of formal education; having refused to utilize a four year academic scholarship because it was not the school of his choice, lacked self confidence, fortitude and determination. He had further acquired proficiency in tailoring, cabinet making, upholstering and may other uncertified skills that many African Americans dreamed to have and envied, during those years. Certainly there had to be an answer, a viable solution for herself and children to rise above our father's fixated condition. Not possessing the magical wand to "awaken" him, she chose to fixate herself into a state of hopelessness and despair.

Our father announced one day that he was scheduled for an interview with a major department store in Detroit as a tailor. This immediately sparked a new sense of hope for our mother. The interview went well and it was pretty much established that he had the job. He was called in the next day and told that they had decided at the last minute not to fill the position with orders from Headquarters. The Head Tailor took him to the side and openly told him that he wasn't hired because he was "colored".

Quite disheartened and experiencing yet another defeat, his already shallow coping skills grew even weaker. His drinking problem got worse, consequently missing more and more time from his job. It got to a point where he hardly went to work at all, and when he did, his earnings were spent in the neighborhood bar. Very often his frustrations were misdirected upon our mother inflicting severe mental and physical abuse upon her which was always observed by the children.

Overwhelmed by the magnititude of her existing condition, our mother's depression led into brief nervous breakdowns, often necessitating hospitalization. These hospitalizations prompted regular weekly psychiatric therapy sessions. As our father's work habits became more and more inconsistent, our mother was compelled to apply for public assistance. This assistance was not nearly sufficient to maintain a household because it was taken into consideration that our father was gainfully employed and did reside with his family. However, a part-time housekeeper was provided to assist with housekeeping and care of the children.

As our mother's mental status regressed with hospital stays increasing, the older children automatically assumed the responsibility of caring for the younger ones. Bunnie had simply become our mother at only 12 years of age and could manage a household as well as any adult. Little Mark clung to her and depended on her so, for she was truly his mother for the time being. On days when the housekeeper was off, the older children took turns missing school to watch over the little ones. Yet they managed to continue to do well in school. Bunnie recalls on one occasion that Frankie, the fifth oldest child who normally did not watch over the little ones, was chosen to because Buddy did not want to miss his swimming match. Frankie was given full instructions on how to care for the little ones and explicit orders not to put their good clothing on them. Naturally he agreed to follow through with all instructions, yet he had a reputation of doing as he pleased. Of course they rushed home at the end of the day knowing that "you now who" was watching the little ones. As had expected, the little one's were all dressed up in their Sunday best. She especially recalls Mark's attire that our father had recently made; a black velvet romper suit with a white peter pan collar, white high top shoes and "no socks", which he looked so adorable in. Of course the older ones wanted to rough Frankie up a bit, however Mark's attire saved him.

Things remained rather bleak for our family. Yet we were managing to hang in there, primarily because of the strong bond that existed among the children. The year is 1951 and our mother continues to see her therapist weekly with hopes that she would strengthen to take charge of her life and the lives of her children. One day while attending her therapy session she openly expressed that she could not deal with her living conditions and our father's physical abuse any longer. She began screaming and crying and couldn't stop. It was diagnosed by the attending psychiatrist that she had suffered a complete nervous breakdown and was transferred directly to Ypsilanti State Hospital for an unspecified length of stay.

The older children were basically told what had happened and that our mother needed rest to get better. Assuming that it would be a lengthy stay, the Michigan Department of Social Services assigned a full time housekeeper to assist with our care.

Our father, experiencing much guilt and inability to cope with the total situation, preoccupied himself with drinking daily. He simply stopped going to work when he didn't feel up to it. Ms. Clark, the housekeeper was a very caring and spiritual woman. She would often take her own money to feed us when our father failed to work or bring home his earnings when he did. Our father would visit our mother regularly in the hospital assuring her that he just needed a little time and things would get better. Almost a year had passed and our mother was still in the hospital. The older children were assured that she was getting better, yet she needed more rest.

It was discovered in July of 1952 that our father had not paid the rent for several months when we were evicted with all of our belongings placed on the street. This wasn't our first eviction, so the older children weren't too alarmed. Our grandmother was contacted and came over to get our belongings. She stated that she didn't have the room to take us in. Our father was in one of the neighborhood bars hiding, Bunnie recalls. Neighbors took us off the streets into their homes for the time being. Ms. Clark notified our mother and the Department of Social Services. Our mother managed to get a temporary release from the hospital and feeling that she had no other recourse decided to place us in foster care through the Michigan Department of Social Services under the supervision of the Children's Aid Society of Detroit. Of course we were assured that this was only temporary until our mother was strong enough to be released from the hospital.

Bunnie vividly recalls the beautiful hot sunny mid-July day of 1952. We were placed in foster care in the following manner: Bunnie, age 13, Kitty age 11, and Cornel, age 3, were all placed with the LaFleurs in River Rouge, MI. Buddy, age 12, Frankie, age 8, were both placed with the Pattersons in Southwest Detroit. Michael, age 6, was placed by himself with the Perrys in Delray, Michigan. Myself (Winnie) having just turned 5 years old was placed in Detroit by myself with a foster mother who's name no one recalls, and Mark, age 2, was placed by himself in Inkster, Michigan with the Young family.

The foster mother with whom I was placed was so abusive that my grandmother managed to have me placed within a month with my older sisters Bunnie and Kitty, and brother Cornel at the LaFleurs.

Bunnie recalls our reactions to this traumatic event: "All of the older kids were grief stricken, the little ones were too young to know what was going on, yet were frightened. I cried for two months non-stop at the thought of us being separated like this with our family being literally "ripped apart.""

It was originally planned that Mark being the youngest of the siblings would be placed in the foster home with the oldest girls. However, due to some mix up within the agency placement procedures, Mark ended up in a foster home in Inkster, Michigan instead of Cornel. I often wonder how things would have turned out for both Mark and Cornel if they had been placed as originally planned, as we are now challenging that past's future.

Mr. and Mrs. Young were well receptive of Little Mark's addition to their family. They were a middle aged couple with a warm and plesant mannerism, awaiting a foster child still in the baby stage as Mark, who was barely 2 years old. They also had another foster child, a boy who was about 2 years Mark's senior.

My older sisters and brothers remained traumatized by the disintegration of our family, and even more so at just the thought of the baby being separated from us again and "alone". This only resulted in them experiencing intense grief, sadness, anger, anxiety and depression. In late August, approximately a month following our separation, Buddy and Frankie were told by their foster parents that Bunnie, Kitty, Cornel, and myself were living with a family in River Rouge, which was just across the street from Southwest Detroit where they lived. They began a relentless pursuit on their bikes to find us. One day shortly after, they found us, with my sister Bunnie recalling, "there are no words that could express that heart warming occasion". Following the hugs, kisses and celebration, it was established that Mark had to be located. Fortunately Buddy and Frankie assured Bunnie and Kitty that their foster parents had connections and would be able to locate Mark, and that they would also see him. Well it turned out that they weren't just boasting. Mark was located and we all got permission to see him through the gracious efforts of the Pattersons.

Bunnie recalls Mark being very happy to see us and it was apparent that he hadn't forgotten us. He still displayed his quiet, passive mannerism. She was further pleased with his living surroundings, which seemed comfortable and caring, with the Youngs assuring us that we could visit our baby brother as often as we wished.

By this time Mike was located in Delray, Michigan. He had as much freedom as Buddy and Frankie with his foster parents being very warm and hospitable. Bunnie, now feeling that her siblings were safe and relatively stable ceased her daily crying spells, which she thought would never end.

Fortunately we were all placed with foster parents who were quite emphathetic regarding the issue of our biological family disruption. They permitted sibling visitation as often as could be arranged. Indeed, my older siblings took full advantage of this emphathetic and caring quality, for it was the key to us maintaining a distant family bond.

Visiting Mark regularly was of grave importance to the older ones which was made known to their perspective foster parents. It was arranged that the Pattersons would take us to see Mark at least every 3-4 months. Of course this wasn't near often enough to permit adequate bonding with the "baby" of the family, yet it was better than not seeing him at all. Our Maternal Grandmother and oldest sister "Yetive" who lived with our grandparents would also visit Mark as often as they could get transportation to Inkster.

My older siblings recall Mark as adjusting relatively well during his early years in foster care. He was rather passive and quiet, yet played and interacted well with other children. His foster parents often stated that Mark was "a pleasant and obedient child". Now that he was talking it was well pronounced that he was tye-tongued. This didn't appear to interfere with his ability to communicate or express himself. It was obvious that the Youngs had become quite fond of Mark. The thought of him being adopted was frightening to my older sisters and brothers. Bunnie recalls that they always made it a point to remind the Youngs that we were a very close family and that our mother would soon be out of the hospital to get our family back together.

Upon our mother's release from Ypsilanti State Hospital, she started visiting Mark regularly. He was now five years old and she recalls him initially not knowing who she was which was quite disturbing to her. After several visits with him he began to understand that she was his mother. He was rather confused about having two mothers and the overall concept of foster care. She further recalls his foster mother being very concerned about his poor eating habits. He just didn't seem to desire any types of food including "sweets" which she found rather peculiar. This lack of desire for food products remained evident throughout his life. However, he did like school very much and did well in his studies. He also enjoyed going to Sunday School and church, loved dressing up, and displayed more interest in his spiritual teachings than the typical 7 or 8 year old.

At the age of around eight during a Bible study session, Mark began to ask the teacher who God and Jesus were, where they came from, who made them, and what color they were. During this questioning period he drew a picture of Christ and colored his face black. He then stood up and displayed his drawing to the entire Bible study class, stating that this was Jesus and that he could be only one color, "black". The teacher proceeded to explain that Jesus was of no specific color, yet Mark insisted that this was not true. Feeling that Mark was being disruptive and disobedient the teacher called his foster mother to come get him. Of course, Ms. Young was quite shocked about all of this, with even her explanations not sufficient enough to change Mark's belief regarding the Jesus he had come to know. Mark's artisitc ability was certainly discovered on that occasion, not to mention the firmness of his developing ego.

With all of the younger children growing up and becoming more integrated into society and the world of reality, we all began to question a lot of things, especially why we didn't live together as a family. Unfortunately, Mark did not have the comfort of daily reassurance by the older siblings that we would be together as a family again, as myself and the other younger kids. It wasn't until family visitations were finally arranged around year 1958 when we all would come together as a family 2 to 3 times a year, that Mark could receive some reassurance.

By this time my oldest brother Buddy was living with our grandparents and shortly after joined the Navy. Bunnie had graduated from Romulus High with a 4.0 grade point average and obtained employment at the Children's Aid Society as a Secretary. For a short period she also lived with our grandparents yet soon got an apartment of her own. Mark was no longer the baby. There was a new addition to the family, the twins "Horace and Freddy", who were now 4 years of age, fathered by my mother's common-law husband, Bill. In view of our mother's continuous problems with inadequate coping skills, the twins had also been placed in foster care at around 6 months of age.

We were still encouraged by the older siblings not to give up the hope of living together as a family again. I especially recall Kitty guiding Cornel and I each night in prayer "asking God to release us from foster care and to bring us back together as a whole family". This was when I first learned the Serenity Prayer which didn't make a lot of sense to me then, yet it guides me daily today. She taught us each day to recite it during our prayers and when we encountered difficult moments – "God grant me the serenity to accept the things I cannot change, the courage to change the things I can, and the wisdom to know the difference."

Our first visit together at our grandparents at 1906 West Grand Blvd in Detroit was indeed a blessing from God. Mark was now around 9 years old and I especially remember him because he seemed so different from the rest of us. He had the biggest eyes, which had such a suspicious look about them, watching and staring at everyone. His mannerism appeared too quiet and withdrawn for such a verbal and outgoing family. Of course we asked him why he wasn't talking; his reply, in a very abrupt manner, was that he didn't have anything to say. At one point Mark was staring out of the window and saw a squirrel. He excitedly said to Cornel, "Hey Tanel, I tee a twirl". Cornel, in his usual foolish and playful manner, fell out laughing, however understanding that Mark was telling him that he saw a squirrel. Mark, quite sensitive about his speech problem told Cornel "if he didn't stop teasing him he would hurt him", in a serious tone. My grandfather quickly took charge of the matter, telling Cornel never to tease Mark again about his speech problem and Mark to never threaten his brother again about anything. We discovered from that point that Mark was truly a no nonsense person.

As our family visits became more frequent, we were able to better understand our individual personalities and respect them as such. Cornel and I were fascinated by Frankie and Michael because they were always boasting about how their foster parents let them visit our family almost every week.

This was the very independence we dreamed to have. Mark didn't seem too moved by our role models; it was as though he had his own unique sense of self and independence. However, he loved coming on home visits and being with his family as much as we all did. Even though Mark didn't have a specific older sibling idol, he developed a very special closeness and bond to Cornel who was two years his senior.

I shall never forget the summer of 1960 at our foster home in Romulus, Michigan, when Cornel at age 11 decided he'd had enough of foster care. He secretly shared with me his plans for running away to our grandparent's home in Detroit. I helped him with the escape plan, for deep inside I wanted out of foster care just as much as he did. We decided to strip his bike of excess weight, fenders etc., so that he could peddle faster and that he would take the only route we knew, the 94 freeway east to the West Grand Blvd exit. I promised him I would tell no one, told him to be careful, hugged him real tight and he was on his way.

As the summer day was ending with the sun setting, my stomach began to ache something awful for I knew I would have to account for Cornel's whereabouts to my foster mother. Upon entering the yard I was immediately asked "where is Cornel"? My reply was that he was still riding his bike. Soon night fell and Cornel was no where to be found. My foster mother insisted that I knew where he was and I insisted that I didn't. Thoughts kept racing through my mind, if he had made it and if he was alright. For some reason deep within I just felt he was o.k. and at our grandparents.

It was now concluded that Cornel was missing and could be in danger so the police were notified. Almost moments after the police were contacted, the phone rang and it was my grandmother in hysterics, repeating over and over, "the child could have been killed". My foster mother was relieved, displaying no anger; I sensed that she was rather happy and contented that Cornel was safe and sound. When I was allowed to talk to Cornel, he told me how the cars on the freeway kept blowing their horns, and how scared he was, but he just kept peddling his bike. He went on to tell me that he had called Mark and told him about the entire runaway episode and how he wanted to pick him up but didn't know how to get to his house in Inkster. Mark explained to him that he could have just taken Michigan Avenue which went directly into Detroit. We really felt rather stupid realizing that our Little Brother had a better sense of direction than we did.

That courageous act on behalf of Cornel seemed to add some light to the end of the tunnel that we so desperately wanted to get to, for on the other side was us together again, living as a family. Over the next few years home visits seemed to be all we looked forward to. The yearning to be together increased with each visit. Kitty had graduated from Romulus High School and was living with our mother in Detroit. Frankie and Michael were practically living with our mother and grandparents because they were always there. The only ones really left in foster care were myself, Cornel, Mark and the twins (Horace and Freddy). The twins lived in a foster home within walking distance from our grandparents which allowed them to be visited and get home visits quite often. I often thought, if only Cornel, Mark and myself lived in Detroit, even in foster care, we could be together more frequently.

Through my ingenious ability, I was able to get our foster parent's foster care license revoked due to their involvement in some illegal activity. Part of our wish came true; Cornel and I were placed in foster homes in Detroit within walking distance from our grandparents. Mark was still in Inkster, yet Cornel and I were determined to get him to Detroit one way or another. Being in Detroit, provided for myself a sense of physical and spiritual closeness to my biological family. My new foster mother was a very kind, generous and compassionate woman, allowing me to visit my family every week. I was even given the priviledge of attending my faith of origin Episcopalian. Every Sunday I attended St. Cyprian's Episcopal Church with my family. I even chose to take the long route to Northwestern High to stop off at my grandparents, before and after school daily. My daily activities were so well planned that most of my friends thought I lived with my grandparents, for being in foster care was indeed a curse, and quite embarrassing.

Mark was now visiting at least twice a month through the persistent efforts of Cornel and me. Naturally we boasted to him about how we were able to visit as often as we chose and how we would visit the twins every week. We further convinced him that the only way he was going to get out of Inkster was to start acting out and demand to be placed in Detroit with the rest of us. Well, our encouragement sessions with Mark must have worked. One day his foster mother called, sharing with our grandmother that Mark was getting hard to manage, talking back, etc., and felt that he should be in a home closer to his brothers and sisters in Detroit. Shortly after, Mark was placed in a foster home in Highland Park on Chandler Street, not quite walking distance to our grandparents, but close enough.

This new sense of freedom for the younger kids was the ultimate blessing from God, and I mean truly a blessing. Though we had been severed as a family from childhood, this grand reuniting was as though we were pieces of a master puzzle having now been located and put into each perspective place. "How amazing!"

Indeed it was amazing that we finally were in close distance of each other yet it wasn't the absolute closeness that we yearned so intensely for; "to live together under one roof".

It became quite evident that the senior family members could/would not retrieve us from foster care. The only logical alternative left was to remove ourselves, just as Frankie and Michael had done. Cornel left first, insisting he wasn't going back to his foster home, with our grandfather finally agreeing to sign the custody papers. My transition was a bit smoother. I had established a good rapport with my foster mother and social worker, and had no doubts that Daddy wouldn't sign the custody papers because I was one of his favorites. What an accomplishment we thought we had achieved.

This left Mark and the Twins still in foster care. We knew if we worked on our grandfather a bit, Mark would be released soon; and we had heard that our mother now living in Rochester, New York with the Twin's father, was working on getting custody of them.

Life with our grandparents was far from the ideal American Dream family. Instead, it was the "real" dysfunctional, yet functional, family life "I" would not have exchanged for any alternate living arrangement. One unique quality that I discovered in that household daily was genuine laughter and joy which took almost three-fourths of my childhood to experience and appreciate. My grandparents were a living riot. "I Love Lucy" was an amateur comedy show compared to them. The very thought of some of the things they used to say and do makes me chuckle uncontrollably within. "My, how I miss those days!"

Mark was now visiting several days throughout the week, with our grandfather always asking him if he had gotten permission, with his reply always being, "yes", knowing that he hadn't. Not a whole lot had changed about Mark now that he was almost 14, except that his speech had really improved. His personality remained quiet and reserved and "oh so serious", with us referring to him as "the little old man". I recall him saying in his abrupt manner, 'I am tired of being in a foster home", without a single word following that statement. He knew Mama (grandmother) had been literally begging Daddy (grandfather) to sign custody papers for him and it seemed as if the old man wasn't budging this time. Well,

Cornel and I knew what the "little old man's" next move would be. Besides, what other choice did he have?

Soon after, Mark came by one day with baggage and all, explicitly stating he was not going back to his foster home ever. Mama began her usual pleading to Daddy, "we've got to take the Little Fellow", with Daddy firmly stating, "he wasn't taking any more of Birt's kids", and that he would have to go to Rochester where she was. Mark's huge eyes burst with tears. I refused to repeat the verbal lashing Mama bestowed upon Daddy following that decision. Going to Rochester didn't really coincide with Mark's plans of being with us, yet he was now through with foster care. We assured him that he wouldn't be in Rochester long; Mama just needed some time to work on Daddy. Custody of the twins was finalized, so Mark had the honor of escorting his little brothers by train to Rochester, New York.

Mark adjusted to Rochester relatively well. He became quite close to our mother and grew very fond of her. It was during this period that he began to voice and display his innate responsibility to watch over and protect his mother and the rest of the females in his family. Indeed we had given him the right title of "Little Old Man". My mother recalls Mark during his stay in Rochester as a loving and respectful teen. Mark was very selective with his choice of friends because he just wasn't attracted to the typical teen activities of the day; smoking, drinking, drugging, and rowdiness. I recall him telling us how awfully sick he became when he tried drinking for the first time and how he just couldn't understand how we could drink alcohol. That experience kindled his beliefs about alcohol and drugs in the years to come. So from age 14 through almost 16, Mark was preoccupied with adult like behavior. He insisted upon wearing suits to school daily, drove an automobile on a regular basis, read current events and regularly debated about serious subject matters. It was as though he was unaffected by the explosion of the rock and roll craze and all that it entailed, that had so greatly affected the vast majority of the youth during the mid sixties.

Mark returned to Detroit in November 1965 for our grandfather's funeral, explicity announcing upon arrival that this was his ticket back to Detroit and that he wasn't going back to Rochester, New York. As much as he would miss being with our mother, he shared that Rochester was just to dull of a City for him. Daddy's death was quite difficult for us all, especially for me because he had sustained a cerebral hemmorage while I was asleep. My grandmother found him the next morning when she arrived from work. She blamed me for a long time afterwards for his death because she felt I should have been more alert and observant. I was in a deep sleep that night, as though I was comatose and just couldn't wake up. Besides I was pregnant and the thought of Daddy finding out put me in a state of depression. How could I possibly tell him that I wouldn't be attending Tuskegee Institute in January as planned.

After the funeral, Mama announced that she wouldn't be able to manage the upkeep of the house by herself and that she would be moving in temporarily with our oldest sister until senior housing was available for her. We all pleaded with Mama to keep the house and apply for Public Assistance since none of us was of legal age to do so, yet she made about a thousand excuses for not being able to. It would have simplified things if she had just admitted that she didn't want the responsibility any longer.

Soon thereafter I married and through the graciousness of my mother-in-law, she took Mark and Cornel in until they were able to secure supervised independent living. Their state social worker was able to obtain them housing and supervision with a kind middle-aged woman on Chicago Blvd. Mark was now age 16 and Cornel was 17, both still greatly needing adult supervision and guidance. One major condition of this supervised independent living status was that they had to be actively enrolled in an educational institution pursuing a high school diploma or its equivalent. Mark was enrolled in regular day school at Central High and Cornel in night school. I certainly was pleased with their new living arrangements because they were in a positive living environment and appeared happy and content for the time being. Thinking about all that we had gone through since the initial disruption of our family - I wanted nothing but the best for my younger brothers for I loved them so dearly.

Obtaining a sound education was a family value that I adopted very early in life, and now that I was approaching young adulthood I constantly emphasized the importancce of educational achievement to my younger brothers. I am certain that this encouragement was effective because they were now attending school regularly and seemed quite sincere about obtaining a high school diploma and going further to college.

Mark really liked the school he was now attending, Central High. He was quite inspired about being a part of a Student Body that were primarily from black affluent families. Central High was located in an area of Detroit's west side where prominant blacks were securing homes/property and businesses with the objective of developing an affluent black community. These noted black families during this time were referred to as "elites". Mark began to blossom, appearing less introverted, becoming more sociable and establishing friends at Central high. It was here that he met his best and dearest friend John H., who became like a blood brother in the years to come.

The struggle for Black Americans was well pronounced among select black students at various educational institutions throughout the country during this period. Around 1967, Mark, taking a special interest in the betterment of black people joined the "Association of Black Students" at Central High. This initial commitment marked the beginning of his "relentless" efforts in the struggle for equality for Black Americans.

During the Detroit 1967 Riots, while many black youth were preoccupied by looting and overall riot activities, Mark was more concerned about spreading the word about the riot, its "purpose" and the message that it intended to convey to White America. Further, that it was only the beginning of what would follow in the continued struggle for equal rights and opportunities for "our" people. It was now quite evident through daily conversations with my brother regarding his genuine beliefs in the movement/struggle that this had become the focal point of his life. He was forever saying that the Movement was the most important thing in his life. My other brothers and I did not doubt Mark's commitment yet we often told him that he was living in a dream world.

I shall never forget when Mark planned a walk-out demonstration at Central High in recognition of our great leader, Malcolm X, and invited Cornel and I to take part. Well, when Cornel and I got to Linwood and Webb, we witnessed almost every black student at Central marching down Linwood Avenue chanting "Malcolm X". Now that Mark was age 17, he was taken to jail for "inciting a riot"; might I add the most peaceful riot I had ever witnessed. Later that day, he was released from jail with charges pending. I certainly learned from that experience that Mark Bethune was far from a "joke".

John H., who Mark met at Central High, had now also joined the Movement and whenever you saw one you saw the other. Their friendship had truly grown into a brotherhood. Mark had expressed his feelings on numerous occasions regarding a white statue of Jesus erected in front of the Sacred Heart Catholic Seminary located on Linwood Avenue and Chicago Blvd as being a false replica displayed within a Black community. So he decided, with John H. fully agreeing that this statue must finally display the true identity of Jesus, "a black man". Later that night Mark and John H. climbed over this huge fence and with Mark being the artist assumed the honor of painting the body parts of the statue with black enamel paint. Not soon after, hardly to their surprise, it was discovered that the statue had been repainted white. Of course Mark painted it again with black enamel paint. Well as far as I can remember it has remained black to this very date. Mark and John H. often boasted about this victory of the struggle.

Displeased with the educational inequalities that existed within the Detroit Public School system for black youth, Mark decided to enroll at "The Free School", which offerred to black youth many educational opportunities that were non-existent within the Detroit Public Schools. Such opportunities were African History, cultural awareness/pride and dignity, productive coping skills and self discipline training, positive mental/physical health and nutrition classes and training. Unfortunately many black parents and families felt that the "free schools" were encouraging care free living and militant attitudes thus assisting the "status quo" to deem the schools unfit for accreditation. The free school concept is now what is referred to today via the Detroit Public School System as Schools of Empowerment; Malcolm X Academy, Marcus Garvey Academy, Erma L. Henderson Institute, etc. They are now schools of choice with astronomical enrollment lists.

Mark was not only a student at the free school, for he assisted diligently with its development, operations, promoting its goals/objectives and recruiting black youth.

During this period, Mark met a man who became a mentor to John H. and him. He often referred to his mentor as the father he never had. When not in school he was receiving further education and training from his mentor in preparation for the struggle. I cannot recall a day that I did not see Mark during this period. When he came he shared his teachings whether I cared to listen or not. When he completed his lecturing for the day, he would always say - "The struggle is calling me - I'll see you tomorrow"; never forgetting a kiss on the cheek and a secure hug. As he would walk away with his arm extended in mid air with a tightly clinched fist, he'd forcefully chant - **"All Power To The People." "All Power To The People."**

Ibo Omar 5

"Mama, tell me all you know about our family's African history, especially how we were captured and forced into slavery; and, Mama, how did you end up with white folks hair, skin color, and features; it was rape wasn't it?" "Those treacherous devils", said Mark. "Son, don't talk so angry and bitter. I am proud of my African ancestry and history and don't you ever forget that I am more African within than you could ever see on the outside", said Mama (our maternal grandmother). We all loved to hear Mama tell stories about the past and the old days, with lots of jokes and laughter; but this time as she spoke, she displayed a sense of firmness and seriousness we'd never seen before.

My mother, Berta Elizabeth Ashford, was of African decent, who's ancestors are from the IBO tribe of Nigeria, Africa, which is one of the most affluent tribes of Nigeria. As they were captured by the white folk and put on slave ships to America, many, many of them jumped overboard and fed themselves to the alligators rather than subject themselves to enslavement. "Your ancestors never willingly became slaves to any man; always remember this," said Mama. She went on further to emphasize her pride and dignity as a black woman by sharing with us an experience she encountered in the latter 1940s, while employed at the Royal Oak Theatre as a maid in Royal Oak, Michigan. One day when she didn't have a baby sitter for our oldest sister Yetive, she decided rather than to miss a days work, she would take Yetive to work with her. When she arrived and was preparing for work, her boss asked her, "Eula, who's pretty little negro child are you looking after". Mama, straight forwardly, replied, "this pretty little negro child is mine". Naturally her boss thought she was just joking, yet Mama insisted that she was indeed her child. "Eula, you're not negro are you?", said her boss. Mama replied, "Yes I am." With numerous apologies her boss replied, "Eula, I'm sorry you can't work here anymore; we just don't employ negros". Mama said she never attempted to pass for white. They just assumed that she was and she never bothered to tell them that she wasn't. Mama went on to share with Mark, as most of us knew, that her father, "Lewis Lepold Gunnthier", was of French and Indian decent yet she loved him as equally as she did her mother.

Mark went on to tell Mama that this was why he had become a black militant. He further proudly announced that he was an official member of The Black Panther Party and that his main purpose in life was to fight for the liberation of his people. Certainly Mama was concerned about his safety in respect to his involvement with the "struggle", yet she fully supported his efforts. For several hours, Mama continued to share with us many significant things about our foundation and African ancestry. Another reality that deeply angered Mark greatly was that Mama's grandmother was the "master's child" as Mama simply put it. Mark simply put it, "our great great grandmother's mother was another victim of plantation rape". It was on this day in early 1969 that Mark decided that he could no longer disgrace himself by bearing his slave name; that he would be known from this day forward as "Ibo Omar", bearing the name of the African Tribe he descended from with honor and dignity.

From this point Mark became officially known in the activist/movement circle as "Brother Ibo". He quite frankly insisted that his family members also refer to him as Ibo, yet thinking from a "negro perspective", we failed to honor his request with sincerity. This truly agitated Mark greatly yet he would say that he understood that our minds were still in chains "enslaved" like the vast majority of black people in America. Realizing this to be a fact he began to put forth more intense efforts with his daily teaching sessions and speaches to liberate the minds of his family members. My older sisters really challenged Mark's need to change his birth given name. They could see no great impact it would have upon his chosen role to liberate his people. His eloquent reply to this challenge was, "Mark Clyde Bethune is my slave name. I am no longer a slave - I have found my true identity - my mind is liberated. Now I face the daily struggle of helping others do the same, especially my biological family members."

The operations of the "free school had virtually come to a stand still and Mark was without a high school diploma or equivalency, by standards of the Detroit Public School system. Aware that he had no other choice but to adhere to such standards he successfully passed the GED equivalency at the Urban League. Furthering his education was also of extreme importance to him. He decided that he would enroll in Wayne State University during the Fall semester. Mark was now living independently in his first apartment on Chicago Blvd. I remember how proud he was having sought my approval prior to moving in. Positive living environemnts were always essential to Mark, free from noise and distraction for he was an advant reader and deep thinker.

Soon after moving into his new apartment, I received a call from Mark stating that he had been arrested coming from his apartment and was being charged with armed robbery. I immediately went to the police station with my Aunt, confirmed the charges and was told he would be arraigned in the morning. The next day he was released on bond. The first thing I asked him was if he was guilty of the charges. He was quite insulted that I would even doubt his innocence. He went on to tell us that the man he was accused of robbing lived in his apartment building and he could think of nothing other than that he was being framed. It was certainly known to the police department that he was a militant activist, and official member of S.N.C.C. (Student Non-Violent Cooordinating Committee) and the Black Panther Party which had merged. "Of course", Mark said, "you know they feel that we are a threat to this country and that we are Communist trying to overthrow the government." Black militant activists were feared greater perhaps than any group of people in this country during this period and were certainly labeled as "criminals". Knowing my brother and for what he stood, I immediately believed that he was being framed. Also, knowing this, we as his family were always afraid that he was a direct target for police harrassment, brutality, and even homicide.

I could look in Mark's huge eyes and tell that he was quite worried and fearful of the trumped up, yet serious charge that was being brought against him. He then very firmly stated, "I didn't rob that man and I will not rot in any white man's jail". Mark's mentor and his dear friend John H. also quite disturbed about this whole matter, assured him that they would secure a good defense attorney. They also emphasized the importance of Mark maintaining his self confidence and self control. Mark, now bearing the distinct militant activist appearance, a well defined afro, earring in one ear, and a dashiki, was furious when he was told by those assisting with his defense that this identity had to subside until the trial proceedings were over. He was "reluctantly" willing to remove his dashiki and the earring from his ear, but cutting his afro off was out of the question. We were able to finally convince Mark, and I mean with a lot of effort and pleading, that he could always grow another afro, but he might not have another chance to hold on to his freedom. Unfortunately, activist groups that were more assertive and forceful in nature in reference to the struggle/movement were not only feared and condemned by the "status quo", but also by many of "our own" misinformed people. Thus Mark could not take the chance with one of those misinformed "negros" on the jury casting the one vote that would render a guilty verdict.

During this period Mark expressed himself as feeling like he was bound and gagged and shackled in chains. He felt so meaningless to the struggle. I was probably more worried about Mark than he himself. I wanted to be of more support to him but I just didn't thoroughly understand the overt political overtone of this so called judicial process, so I just had to entrust my brother's life within the hands of those who did. On the day of the examination a strange thing happened, yet not unexpected. The plaintiff failed to show up, so the charges were dropped, and my, what a celebration we had. Mark vowed that he would wear a skull-cap until his afro grew back. He must have asked me a thousand times daily, "Winnie, does it look like its growing?" I would reply, "Yes, Mark", cracking up inside. I would have not ever let him see me laughing, for he still remained so sensitive. A week or so later, Mark saw the black guy who accused him of robbing him. He admitted that he had been bribed by some detectives of the Police Department to set Mark up. He further shared that he didn't show up for trial because he just couldn't go through with it. Mark came to my apartment that same day and shared this with me. I went back to his place on Chicago, a short distance from where I lived, and met this guy. He admitted to me also that my brother had not robbed him and shared how bad he felt. Mark summed it up as being another aspect of the struggle to which he had dedicated his life.

I always wondered when Mark was going to give himself a break from the Movement - party a little, get himself a girlfriend. One day he brought by this very attractive young lady with a beautiful smile and a gorgeous afro. He introduced her as being Suncreeya and how beautiful he thought she was and how crazy he was about her. This was the first time he had ever brought a young lady by and introduced her in such a manner, so I knew he was quite serious about her. All of my brothers were good looking and had "ladies for days", but not Mark - he was strictly a one lady's man. Suncreeya was still in high school, almost 17 years old and had joined the Movement. She told me how Mark insisted that he give her an African name; that no woman of his would represent him with a slave name. So calling her Suncreeya came natural because this was the name she was introduced as. Addressing Mark as Ibo, at the time seemed so unnatural unless my brothers and I were joking about, "Ibo".

Mark fell deeply in love with Suncreeya, it was as though he worshipped her. I hadn't seen him that serious since joining The Movement. Actually, our family was quite concerned about his devotion to this girl. Suncreeya's father disliked Mark with a passion and forbade his daughter to have any dealings with him. Their relationship grew dispite her father. Mark was not allowed to call her home, so I was elected as the mediator until her family found out that I was

Mark's sister. Naturally he couldn't go to her home, so they always had to meet somewhere. Then Suncreeya became pregnant with Mark's child. He insisted that she do nothing to interrupt the pregnancy. I truly believe she wanted this child, however, her mother found out and the pregnancy was terminated. Mark became so overwhelmed with grief, anger, and hurt that I thought he'd never pull himself together. Yet he did. He then decided that he and her father needed to have a man to man talk. He went to her house. He didn't get very far with the father. When he got back to my apartment he had been seriously beaten with a bat by her father. It was later discovered at the hospital that he had a fractured rib, along with severe abrasions. We went directly to our Aunt's house on LaSalle Boulevard after leaving the hospital. Our Aunt was hysterical when she saw Mark's condition. She kept saying that she knew that something like this would happen if he kept pursuing this girl. We all came to the conclusion that Mark would simply have to deal with his feelings and terminate his relationship with Suncreeya to cease any further self destruction. I could identify with the hurt in him because I knew how much he loved her. I had to support him getting over her and I was certain that he could.

The brothers and sisters in the struggle were certainly helpful with giving him extra support during this period. They knew that nothing and no one could entice him to abandon The Movement. I am quite certain that Suncreeya was aware of this. Mark's involvement with The Movement remained as active as always. There were certainly ongoing incidents within the City of Detroit, not to mention the entire country during this period that warranted activist involvement. One such incident was the aftermath of the "New Bethel Incident", where two young black males were on trial for the alledged murder of one Detroit Police Officer and the wounding of another in March of 1969. In recalling the incident, the Republic of New Africa was having a meeting at the New Bethel Church on Linwood Avenue. Alledgedly, two Detroit Police Officers were shot when they stopped to question a group of black men standing outside the church with rifles. From that point, back up officers were called and a shoot out occurred. Police officers then entered the church, firing their guns, shooting over the heads of men and women and into the walls, with everyone on the floor trying to get to the basement of the church. Later, over 100 men and women occupants of the church were locked up for seven hours without food, water, or toilets, until former Recorder's Court Judge George Crockett ordered them to be released. Mark was now working diligently on behalf of the defense of the two young black males being charged with the alledged murder and wounding of the two involved Detroit Police Officers. One of the young men being charged resided with Mark for a period during the trial proceedings. The young man originated from the East Coast. Mark made it a point to introduce the young man to all of his family members, for he truly believed in his innocense. I recall him as being extremely knowledgeable and politically intellectual. He totally denied the charges stating that he wasn't even in Detroit during the incident and felt that he was being targeted because of the specific status that he held within the Republic of New Africa. Both of the young men being charged were later acquitted of the charges. Mark concluded these not guilty verdicts as still another victory for the struggle. He further concluded that the New Bethel incident, because of its serious nature and blatant racial overtones, would become a historical event of the struggle for "our people".

It was now mid 1970 and Mark has also become a leading member of the A.A.P.U. (All African People's Party). His overall dedication to the liberation of his people was well pronounced at this point. He was residing in a real nice flat on Stoepel in Detroit. It seemed like every time I would visit him, he was always decorating, using basic colors, especially black, because that was his favorite color. He just simply didn't like bright colors. Cornel used to ask him, "Man, why do you wear black so much? People will think you're wearing the same clothes everyday". Mark would simply reply, "because that's what "I" like". Black seemed to compliment his no nonsense, strictly business attitude and overall mannerism. It was here on Stoepel that I vividly remember how knowledgeable Mark had become. This knowledge having been acquired through reading extensively and being amidst enriching environments. He would often mention, while lecturing one on one to me, his great concern about me letting my intellect go to waste with daily usage of alcohol and being in inferior environments. "You've got to start feeling better about yourself and build your self esteem - just think, you're even a gifted singer; you should be going in the direction of Nina Simone, Nancy Wilson, Sarah Vaughn - How could you let such gifted talent go to waste?", he'd say. I would always agree with what he was saying, giving some flimsy excuse that I was going to get my life together sooner or later. Actually I felt quite ashamed that my little brother so often would bring to my attention my lack of fortitude during those days to live up to my potential. As he put it, my enchained mind had me at a stand still. Though my mind was indeed enchained, for some strange reason I have been able to retain a fair amount of Mark's vital teachings. It disheartens me so when I check my memory bank to discover so much that has been lost through my previous years of destructive living.

Perhaps the most important thing that I learned from his teachings is that capatilism is simply based on supply and demand. During that period we as blacks in America were doing much of the demanding and supplying little or nothing, consequently reaping little or no benefits. He always talked about J. Paul Getty, then referred to as the wealthiest man in the world, who concluded that land and oil is both wealth and power. Indeed he possessed a vast amount of both. He would lecture about the works of Mao Tse Tung and specifically how he eliminated the heroin epidemic in Red China by simply providing two alternatives: recovery or death. He was indeed a profound student of many other noted Revolutionists: Dubois, Fanon, Nkrumah, Cabral, and Che Guevara, to mention a few, and could discuss their works at great lengths. Anyone that knew Mark within the political activist arena was well aware of his articulate lecturing and debate abilities. I recall the day he handed me a book on the works of Mao Tse Tung and instructed me to read it in its entirety. I only read a portion of it, however, I kept it as a keepsake for years and somehow it just disappeared.

Something that we both had in common was a great love for all fields of the arts, literature, paintings/drawings, dance, and yes, "music", my greatest love. I can truly say that this quality was directly inherited from both of our parents, also profound lovers of the arts, not to mention talent; our father a literary scholar and a perfect tenor, our mother an artistic decorator and a dynamic dancer, and certainly they possessed many other artistic abilities. Mark was in tune with my deep love for music, especially jazz, and often he would take me to live jazz performances. One evening he announced that he was taking me out to this lounge on Livernois, which was a few blocks from his flat. "I want you to check out this vocal and instrumental group who has one of the most unique contemporary sounds I've ever heard. Its not jazz, but I know you'll love the sound", he said. Mark was right! I had never heard anything like their sound before. I was spellbound. The year was late 1970, the group - "Earth, Wind, and Fire". I would often brag about them and how my little brother turned me on to the sensational Maurice White/Earth, Wind and Fire before they acquired fame and fortune. Whenever I listen to Earth, Wind, and Fire, Mark automatically comes to my mind because he would say "just listen to the message in their music, Winnie. Isn't it deep?"

My younger brothers and cousins and I would often joke about "Ibo's" conversations and debates being so deep that you needed a Rose 20 (Wild Irish Rose, 20 percent wine) just to sit and listen. I'm serious! Friends would ask us "Does your brother ever give the Revolution a rest?" And we would reply "Ask Ibo. I bet he's got the right answer for you." (smile) One subject matter that Mark did not talk at lengths about was the separation of our family during our formative years. He would simply say that it was totally uncalled for, blamed much of it on the system and the majority of it on our father, whom he equated as being weak and irresponsible. Mark believed that it was our father's duty and responsibility as a black man to have kept his family together at all costs. He totally refused to accept any explanation/excuse our father had given for not having done so. He further expressed much disgust and embarrassment for our father living the life of a derelict, drowning himself in cheap wine daily to cope with the guilt and pain he so deeply felt within. Often I would try to get Mark to look at the total picture and not be so condemning, yet he felt George (our father) was deserving of no more. During this period, George was quite physically and mentally ill and Cornel and I were attempting to get him into the V.A.

Hospital, with hopes that he would soon get his V.A. disability benefits reinstated to improve his overall living conditions. Mark refused to assist us for reasons being, yet he would take me to the V.A. Hospital on occassions to visit him. He would wait in the car until the visit was over. I made many attempts to encourage Mark to see his father, yet he'd only say, "I want no dealings with the man".

The year is 1971 and Marvin Gaye was sending some powerful messages with his "What's Going On" album. Mark was totally spellbound by the messages Marvin Gaye was conveying to the people and America as a whole with this "musical masterpiece". He was so proud of Marvin's political accomplishments with this album that he had it on constant display in his window. "Oh" how I vivdly recall Marvin standing there proudly drapped in a fitted black vinyl trench coat with the collar turned up around his neck with perfection and distinction. A selection from that album "Save The Children", sparked Mark's "Save The Children Campaign". He immediately began devising "Save The Children" banners, posters, and literature to distribute throughout the communities. He openly lectured to the "people" regarding our roles and responsibilities to save our black children from the plight/devastations of drugs, alcohol, poor physical/mental health, poverty, illiteracy, ignorance, hunger, domestic/public violence (powerless and senseless death).

Mark developed a deeper concern regarding the intensity of unhealthy, unsafe, non-productive living environments for children on the East Side of Detroit, spending much time campaigning on the major streets. He also volunteered several hours a day at a recreation center in the Conners and Mack area. He worked diligently with these children in an effort to strengthen their characters in a positive direction, teaching them African history, pride, self discipline, art (drawing/painting) and basic survival skills. During his spare time at the center, he drew a mural on every wall consisting of noted black and those of color revolutionaries/activists and distinguished African Queens and Kings, forever reminding the children to be aware and proud of their heritage. Kitty (our sister), who at that time was teaching in the Rochester, New York Public School System, was quite heavily into African History which she acquired while attending Tuskegee University. Mark was well aware of this. He would often converse with her and express his disappointment in her for not teaching in the inner city schools, which were heavily concentrated with black children, sharing her knowledge, which he felt was her devout duty to her people.

"Positive black role modeling is essential for the proper development of both male and female black children, too much of the opposite are they seeing daily", Mark would say. He made it a point to display positive role modeling to all children with whom he came in contact. A day hardly went by that he didn't spend quality time with his nieces, nephews, and younger cousins. When interacting with them, he was always kind, gentle, considerate and oh, so patient. Terri, my daughter, recalls how often she would see her uncle and how he would take her to those "Black Power" meetings, as she would refer to them, with all those strange people. She even recalls the day he took her to Wayne State University and how they were purchasing lunch in the Student Center Building, when she asked her Uncle Mark why the cashier gave him the same dollar back that he gave her. Her Uncle Mark softly replied, "Baby, we've just liberated lunch". Detroit residents that can recall, I am sure, shall never forget the tragic incident when a five year old black child died one Halloween after eating candy laced with dope. Mark was furious. "Dope must be eliminated one way or the other, because they'll have children using the garbage", he said. Well I am certain that all of us still living today can attest to the validity of that projection.

For some reason or another, Mark decided that he needed different scenery. He announced that he was going to L.A., California to enjoy some of the sunshine and warm weather and try his luck at acting and modeling. Wherever he got this notion I'll never know, other than that there was no challenge too great for him besides believing that he was one of the most handsome black guys in the City. Not knowing how long he would be residing in L.A., he decided not to give up his flat, leaving our brother Cornel in charge of the upkeep. Cornel assured him that everything would be in tact when he returned. When Mark arrived in L.A., he called, stating that he had a safe trip and talked about how beautiful the scenery was. He was thinking about making this his home, depending on how successful his pursuit would be. About a month later he called sharing that he was compiling a picture portfolio for a modeling prospect and would mail us copies of the pictures. The pictures were really great; he looked like a different person with a new perspective on life. Aunt Bessie was hysterical, thinking that he wasn't coming back. She loved Mark and all of her sister's children as equally as she loved her own. Though all of us missed Mark dearly, we were hoping that he had found a career objective aside from The Struggle.

Well, his stay in L.A. only lasted a few months; Mark was coming home, stating that L.A. just wasn't the paradise he thought it would be. I intentionally did not inform him that Cornel had not kept the rent up in his flat as promised and had sold all of his furniture. When Mark found out about his housing situation upon his arrival, he waited patiently at Aunt Bessie's until Cornel showed up, and immediately challenged him to a fight. Cornel refused to fight back, laughing the whole matter off. Mark asked Cornel why he hadn't kept up the rent and Cornel, in his usual foolish manner replied, "If you'd left the money I would have". Naturally we all laughed until we couldn't laugh anymore. Mark was so hurt and disappointed that he was in tears. I tried to console him by reminding him that he knew how irresponsible Cornel was, yet Mark's reply was, "He's my brother; if I can't trust him, who can I trust?" That reply,

I did not dare challenge.

Aunt Bessie's house on LaSalle was large enough for an additional family besides her 11 children, so Mark knew that he wasn't outdoors. Besides, Aunt Bessie's had always been our second home. That day, Mark confirmed that he remained very much a great part of The Movement, with his lecture of the day focused on honesty, respect, love, and dedication for your blood family. Some of the issues he pointed out were right on target. Cornel even shared how awful he felt behind betraying not just his brother, yet his younger brother's trust. Mark went on to announce that he would be paying his older brother Mike a visit real soon since he had now chosen to sell dope as well as continue to use it.

Cornel and I went to the Twenty Grand Motel where Mike and a couple of his friends were dealing (selling drugs). Mike was all decked out in his smoking jacket and talking much "jive" and making jestures that he was indeed "the man". We announced to him that "Ibo" would be paying him a visit real soon regarding his drug selling business. Mike's reply was that he didn't want to hear anything Mark had to say about Black Power and "that struggle" shit. His visit certainly wouldn't be long because he was about making money and he didn't have time for the lecturing. Mike's partners fell out laughing, making statements like "I heard "Ibo" was truly down for the cause". Mike's reply was that "He's doing his thing and I'm doing mine; it's as simple as that".

As Mark had so declared, some days later, he paid Mike

a visit at his place of business, his room in the Twenty Grand Motel. Mike, upon greeting Mark, told him that he wasn't up to any lectures, that this was his life and "The Movement" was his. Mark, overriding Mike's statement, went on to share that it was most unfortunate that he was a victim of the very product he was selling and that he was certain that he was his best customer. Mike specifically shared that the product that he was selling was "mix jive" (inferior grade of heroin)and what he used was raw (quality grade of heroin). However, we all new that Mike would use any form of heroin available to him, depending on the circumstances besides as Mark reminded him "garbage is garbage" with no levels of quality. Mike, further shared that Mark didn't know anything about the dope game and needed to stay out of adult business. Mark replied by sharing that what he did know about the dope game was that it was deadly and that it was going to eventually take his life one way or the other. Further, that it was his desire if he chose to be enslaved by it but no brother of his would sell death as long as he was alive. "Mike, he said, What I mean in simple terms is that you better close your dope house down or I'm going to close it down for you. That's how much I love you." Mike replied, "Man are you threatening me." Mark's final reply was, "No, It's a promise."

Mike's mellow men were definitely taunting him now. "You gonna let your little brother come in here and talk to you like that?" they said. Mike smoothed it off by saying, "that Black Power shit has blown that boys mind". In two days

Mike closed up shop, using some flimsy excuse that the spot he was dealing from had gotten a little hot (anticipating a bust from the Police Department). However, he knew what all of us knew. "Brother Ibo" would have carried out his promise!

Heroin sales and prostitution was perhaps at its peak in the early seventies in the Detroit black ghettos. Although heroin was sold in dope houses, it was evident to adults and children where the dope houses were because of the constant traffic from those that demanded it. It had become so permissable by these inner city communities that young children would witness daily an addict coming from these houses; nodding, scratching, mumbling to self, displaying swollen hands and/or walking briskly to their destination to consume their purchased "death". Residents were actually terrified by the very word "heroin"; so terrified that they believed there was nothing they could do to eliminate its sales/trafficing. The black activist groups were primarily the only ones that displayed the courage and determination to combat the devastation of this destructive deadly product.

It is now the year 1972. Mark continued to work diligently with his Save The Children and Anti-Drug campaigns. Often he would have campaigns/rallys at Aunt Bessie's or directly in front of her house in LaSalle Park. It was amazing how he could really get people stirred up for talking and sharing. One great thing that all of the residents were deeply concerned about was the future of black children and coming to the realization that their future was in our hands and what we did then would certainly determine what their tomorrow would be like. When I look at the status of the young adults today who were children then, I can honestly admit that I did not take his "Save The Children" campaign very seriously not to mention the many other adults at that time that didn't.

Aunt Bessie would be so proud of Mark when he conducted his campaigns or just small lectures to the family. She would always say that he was so bright and intelligent like our father only George lacked that leadership quality that was so vibrant in Mark. Toni, Aunt Bessie's oldest child, and Mark were the same age, yet she really admired and looked up to him. Her perception of her cousin was the ideal black man of the day, especially how he respected and placed the black sister always on a pedastal. Toni was just intrigued by Mark's lectures and involvement in The Movement and was thrilled on occasions when she accompanied him to some important meeting. Those occasions were quite limited because Mark truly abided by the confidentiality of those meetings. He always and only discussed/shared information he felt to be beneficial to our personal growth and nothing more. Our cousin Mario, a bit younger, admired Mark for his bold and daring mannerism; he simply didn't think there was anything Mark couldn't do, and wanted to be just like him. Mark was always telling him how proud he was of his willingness to be part of The Struggle, but he was a bit too young and unprepared.

Mark's stay at Aunt Bessie's was brief, for he always needed his personal space, independence and lots of peace and quiet. He was able to find a roomy bungalow in Highland Park an adjoining city to Detroit. Since he was approaching his 22nd birthday he decided to have a house warming and birthday party combined. It was mandatory that all adult family members attend, in addition to his close friends. That day was rather special. It was chilly, yet sunny with a clear blue sky, with such a pleasant and cheerful atmosphere. Mark didn't do a lot of lecturing that day other than expressing how much he loved his family and pledged to always look after us with emphasis upon the females. He introduced his beautiful puppy "Cocoa" he had recently purchased, who was half Doberman and Shepherd. It was the most gorgeous puppy I'd ever seen with a radiant brownish/black coat. Naturally, Yetive attempted to pry a little regarding some of the confidential aspects of The Movement", yet Mark smoothed it off by saying, "Now sister dear, we don't discuss such matters, especially with the females." Overall that day turned out to be a fantastic 22nd birthday and joyful house warming for Mark.

Mark maintained his firm position regarding the importance and necessity of black children being taught African History, tradition and culture to acquire a better understanding of themselves and their ancestry. Further, to develop rigid self discipline to repell such negative forces as drugs/alcohol, illiteracy, community and family violence and other destructive life patterns. He realized that the vast majority of black children spent much of their day in the Detroit Public School System, thus they should be afforded the opportunity to learn about their enriching culture because it should be included in their standard educational curriculum, especially since black Americans played such an important role in the development and prosperity of this country. Therefore, he campaigned rigorously in hopes that this would soon one day become standard practice in the predominantly black inner city schools of Detroit. Becoming quite frustrated with the outcomes of his campaign, yet always remaining optimistic, he and other activists launched another campaign to get Northwestern High School to change its name to Malcolm X High. Though the name change was never adopted, his and the dedicated efforts of others was quite galant and they were highly recognized as such. There was one event that was implemented during this period that Mark assisted diligently with the development of "Soul Day", which is held yearly during mid August on Northwestern's School grounds to this very date. This event is perhaps one of the first publically recognized African cultural based commemorations held yearly in the City of Detroit.

  Every year during Mother's Day, our mother always came to Detroit to take part in Bunnie's Club's Mother's Day special event celebration. She would usually remain throughout the summer. Mark would always look forward to her coming because we would all gather at Bunnie's house which gave him the grand opportunity to challenge us in endless lectures and debates. Mark had really been lecturing Bunnie and I about taking birth control pills, how they were one of the primary social forms of genocide that we had become victims of. Further, emphasizing that these pills were very dangerous with numerous unhealthy side effects. He used our mother as an example by saying if this form of genocide had been implemented in the minds of black women during her era, Black Americans would be almost extinct by now. We posed the question to him regarding black children being born to parents who were not; economically, physically/mentally, spiritually sound to care for them. Mark responded to this by saying, "There is no such thing as someone within the family or black community unable to properly meet the needs of all black children. In Africa, villages raise children - it is a collective responsibility which through tradition we carried out even on the plantation, however we have allowed white ways of thinking to infiltrate what we "know" we should be doing". It was certainly difficult to argue the merits of Mark's position. We pointed out that this was a lot of idealistic thinking, verses reality. He calmly said to us "that anything perceived can be achieved".

Mark was truly a devout optimist for each goal he set he intended to accomplish and each challenge he met he intended to overcome or win. My niece, Shawn, recalls when she was 9 years old how her Uncle Mark challenged her, her brother Mike and her mother Bunnie in a game of monopoly. At such a young age she remembers how he was determined to maintain his winning status. He continued to loan them monopoly money to prolong the game to continue to win. This game went on for four intense hours.

On another occasion, Mark was lecturing to Bunnie, our mother and me about the revolutionary change that must occur in America for black people to fully become liberated. The white oppressors had the majority of us believing that we were free because we were no longer baring "visible" chains and shackles on "visible" plantations. Now our oppressors had become much more sophisticated by using devices such as heroin, alcohol, birth control, family separation, family violence, illiteracy, unemployment, poverty, police brutality, and homicide to maintain control and power. "I cannot and will not continue to watch the destruction of my people. This is why I am militant and have dedicated my life to The Struggle", he said. Birt (our mother) interrupted him and said, "Mark, that militant talk is going to get you killed". Mark said, "Mother dear, I've got to do what must be done for The Struggle."

That day Mark went on to talk about the irresponsible and inadequate husbands/male partners of the females within our family. He said he had been thinking about purchasing a big house that we could all live in together, therefore he could make sure that his mother, sisters, and nieces and nephews would be properly cared for. Naturally, we thought he was indeed fantasizing, yet he said that he was "dead serious". Actually, I don't know why we didn't take him seriously, because if he didn't come every day to check on us he certainly called each of us and I mean more than once a day.

That summer Mark announced that he had met this beautiful sister whom he had been dating and in his opinion was definitely marriage material. The day I met Rose I looked in Mark's eyes and could tell he had finally fallen in love again. Rose was small and petite, fair complexioned, very attractive and of course wore a lovely afro. Her mannerism was low key and pleasant. She shared that she was very much a part of The Struggle and supported Mark's efforts 100 percent. I kind of got the feeling that this relationship was rather serious on both parts. As time went by whenever I would see Mark, I'd see Rose and they appeared happy, in love, and quite compatible.

During the Summer and Fall of 1972, I spent a lot of meaningful and enjoyable times with Mark. At times he'd be with Rose and then other times, he felt we needed to be together alone to talk some things over between brother and sister. Most of his conversations were about how deeply he loved his family and of course The Struggle. He shared that he had been intensely working on his mission for over a year now to eliminate drugs in the City of Detroit. He insisted that he had a strategic plan and believed it would work. He went on to say that if the source is eliminated then there would be no dope to use, "right?" I would agree saying ,"I guess you're right about that!" Each time I'd ask him about this plan of his he would say "Now Winnie, you know not to ask such questions" - and certainly I knew not to ask - and certainly I finally stopped asking.

A few days before Thanksgiving of 1972 I was sitting with Mark in his bungalow and he shared with me that he was pretty sure that Rose was pregnant with his child and that he was quite happy about becoming a father. I asked him if/when he was planning to marry her and he assured me that it was in the making. I was quite elated to hear that especially knowing how Mark loved and very much wanted children. However, he insisted that nothing would interfere with his mission - that it would be carried out as planned. He then spoke with our oldest brother "Buddy" in New York to remind him that he had some important business to discuss with him when he arrived the day before Thanksgiving. As planned, Buddy went to Mark's place as soon as he arrived to talk privately with him. To this date, I do not know the purpose or contents of that meeting. Buddy only shared that it was a Big Brother - Little Brother heart to heart talk. That which I do know to be a fact is that "no" blood family member saw or talked to Mark after Thanksgiving Day of year 1972 ever again - that is "alive" in the physical sense.

Mama (Grandmother) in her late twenties

Father in his late fifties

Mark at age - 4 with mother

Dies on roof...

ATLANTA—Atlanta Police and firemen lower the body of Mark C. Bethune of Detroit, Mich., from the roof of a Morris Brown College dormitory after being shot to death in a shootout with an Atlanta policeman. Bethune, a fugitive wanted for the slaying of a Detroit policeman, had been hunted in the Atlanta area for four days. There were conflicting reports on how Bethune, 22, died, however. UPI

THE MOTHER OF Mark Clyde Bethune, Mrs. Eulania Brantley (left foreground), of Rochester, N.Y., is escorted through the crowd outside of the Stinson funeral chapel where services for Bethune were held Saturday afternoon.

THE YOUNG, THE OLD, the sorrowing, the curious...whatever their reason they waited patiently outside Stinson funeral chapel while services were being conducted inside for Mark Clyde Bethune, for a look at the cortege that was to carry his body to Detroit Memorial Park for burial.

The Hunt 6

The American Heritage Dictionary's Second College Edition definition of "Hunt" - to pursue for food or sport - to seek out, search for, to search through, as for game or prey. To make use of (hounds, for example) in pursuing game. To drive out forcibly: A diligent and thorough search or pusuit as: the hunt for the escaped prisoner.

It was mid evening in the later part of the week following Thanksgiving of 1972 when the doorbell rang at the home of my sister Bunnie. As she opened the door, she discovered that it was two white detectives, dressed in overcoats and suits flashing their badges, announcing that they were from the Police Department and would like to talk with her briefly about her brother Mark Bethune also known as "Ibo", she then permitted them to enter her home acknowledging that Mark Bethune was her brother. The detectives went on to say that they had reason to believe that Mark was involved in a murder that took place in Highland Park, in an apartment believed to have been rented by Mark Bethune. They proceeded to ask her when she had last seen Mark and Bunnie replied, "Thanksgiving Day". The detectives then asked Bunnie if she had any knowledge of any organization that Mark may have been affiliated with. Bunnie replied that she didn't know of any specific names of organizations but that Mark was quite involved with the Civil Rights Movement for Black Americans. Bunnie went on to say that she could not believe that Mark could be involved with the murder of someone and that all of this had to be a mistake. The detective then said that Mark was not being charged with a crime but that they would like to question him. Bunnie assured the detectives that she would convey the message to Mark as soon as she heard from him. After the detectives left Bunnie recalls feeling simply petrified by what the detectives had shared with her and certainly she felt that the allegations were untrue. In somewhat of a state of shock, she nervously resumed with shampooing the living room carpet and suddenly without any warning, the handle of the shampooer escaped from the grip of her hands and landed on the cocktail table glass, totally shattering it into tiny pieces. While cleaning up what seemed to be millions of pieces of glass, Bunnie concluded that the trauma behind all of this was too overwhelming to share with the rest of the family that day and would deal with it in the morning.

The next day Bunnie received a call from Yetive (our oldest sister) stating that she had just had a visit from two detectives from the Police Department alledging that Mark may be involved in a murder that had taken place at his place of residence. Certainly the both of them were extremely upset over this whole matter yet sincerely believed that this was just a mistake and that Mark would soon show up to clear up these allegations. In the meantime, Bunnie had contacted

Michael and me, who were the only other siblings residing in Detroit at the time to see if we had seen or heard from Mark since Thanksgiving Day and informing us of the police visit and allegations. Of course Mark and Michael barely spoke to each other at Thanksgiving in view of their extreme differences in life styles, which was the last time Mike had contact with him. I was the last family member to converse with Mark prior to him leaving on Thanksgiving Day. When we contacted Aunt Bessie and our first cousins it was discovered that neither of them had seen or talked with Mark since Thanksgiving. I then contacted Frankie, who resided in Ann Arbor, attending the University of Michigan, and he also stated that he hadn't talked to Mark since the family Thanksgiving dinner/gathering. Naturally, we all began to get a bit worried because Mark would never go several days without contacting a family member.

    Shortly following this alarming news from the Police Department, and article was featured in the Local News, naming Mark Bethune as a suspect in the alledged murder of a drug kingpin in the Highland Park area and the kidnapping of his suspected partner/bodyguard who had managed somehow to escape. Through the acknowledgement of Mark's firm position regarding the eradication of drug sales/availability in Black commmunities, we began to contemplate as to whether Mark may be involved with this matter in some way or another. Within my thoughts, the conversation I last had with Mark kept racing through my mind; especially when he shared that the time had come to execute his mission to rid black communities and save black children from the destructive forces of drugs, namely "heroin". Had the mission began, I thought?

It was Dec 4, 1972, various family members were watching the evening news. The newscaster announced that there was a shoot out between Detroit Police Officers and three young black males on Detroit's Northwest side. Further, it was believed that one of the suspects was Mark Clyde Bethune, also being sought in the connection of the murder of an alledged Highland park drug dealer and the kinapping of his partner. Following this announcement, pictures of the alledged suspects were flashed across the T.V. screen and their names - Mark Clyde Bethune, John Percy Boyd, and Hayward Brown. Suddenly the family nightmare began.

<u>The Detroit News, Evening Circulation, December 4, 1972</u>
Headline Reads - **Four STRESS Officers are Shot By Gunmen**

"Four Detroit Police officers, working in plain clothes as members of the department's controversial STRESS Operation, were shot and wounded early today when they stopped a car on Detroit's Northwest side.

The officers returned fire as the car sped from the scene. The bullet-riddled vehicle was found abandoned several blocks away a short time later. Twenty-three persons, including a married couple registered as owners of the car, were taken into custody, either as suspects or possible witnesses.

Police are seeking eight warrants on charges of assault with intent to commit murder. The persons held were arrested in a series of house raids in Northwest Detroit, but officers refused to say what information led to the arrests.

District Inspector James Bannon said preliminary investigation indicated that the shooting was narcotics related and that he did not believe it was connected with any black militant movement. Bannon said the STRESS officers had been watching a suspected narcotics pad on Stoepel, North of McNichols, and followed the Volkswagon after it pulled over the car a few blocks from the house. The wounded officers are: Patrolman Robert A. Rosenow, 23, in serious condition in Henry Ford Hospital, with multiple gunshot wounds; Patrolman Eugene J. Fular, 24, in serious condition; Patrolman Richard D. Grapp, 41, in serious condition; and Patrolman Billy M. Price, 32 in satisfactory condition.

Inspector John Domm, Commander of the Homicide Section, said police were not certain why the officers stopped the car, a white Volkswagon. "We're still trying to piece together a lot of stuff that at the moment doesn't fit in", Domm said.

The Westbound car was stopped on McNichols, just east of Stoepel, a block west of Livernois and the University of Detroit Campus at 1:05 a.m.

Price was shot as he approached the Volkswagon. Fular was shot as he tried to get out of the car; he fell to the pavement. Grapp and Rosenow were both shot inside the unmarked police car.

The officer returned the fire and the car sped away. Patrolman Price shouted into the police car radio for help and within minutes a dozen other police cars were at the scene. The Volkswagon was found abandoned a few minutes later on

Stoepel at Santa Clara, about two blocks north of the shooting scene. The rear windshield was shot out and a bullet had punctured the front left windshield. Six other bullets had pierced the car. Domm said there was no indication that any of the occupants had been struck by police."

STRESS, an acronym for Stop the Robberies - Enjoy Safe Streets, is a police operation designed to place extra officers, some acting as decoys to attract criminals, in high crime areas. The operation was restructured after several STRESS officers were involved in a gun fight last year, with some Wayne County Sheriff's Deputies, in which a Deputy was killed.

I shall never forget how "unreal" this overwhelming news appeared to me. Was there any connection between the allegations brought against my brother regarding the murder of a noted drug dealer and now the allegations of his involvement in a shootout with Detroit STRESS police officers? What was the meaning of these two events? Again, I thought, is the "mission" in process? To rid my mind of unwanted thoughts and my heart of unbearable feelings, I reached to my most comforting and dependent friend - "alcohol" - for what else at that time did I possess that could provide the support I needed to cope with what lie ahead.

Bunnie vividly recalls her reaction to the December 4th STRESS incident allegations compounded by the murder allegations regarding her younger brother as evoking a sudden rush of emotions; fear, embarrassment, denial and desperation, intensely wanting to simply dissolve or escape. At the time, she was employed with the Federal Government, at the U.S. Army Tank-Automotive Command division in Warren, Michigan, and was well liked and highly respected by the high ranking officers to the civilian employees. How would this affect her superb work status, she thought? Bunnie further recalls feeling quite burdened, being second to the oldest, yet forever being looked to for guidance by her younger siblings of such a troubled family. How on earth could this family deal with anymore trauma than it already had? Was it a curse on the Bethune Family? Fortunately, she had devoted and caring friends, especially her club members who would stick by her through thick and thin. As she remembers, numerous friends contacted her upon her brother making news headlines, even friends from childhood, with each of them extending empathy, words of compassion and support. To her discovery, none of her co-workers appeared to know that Mark Bethune was her brother other than close friends who vowed to keep it hush hush, as she had requested of them. From this point, Bunnie realized how blessed she was to have such dedicated friends as a viable means of support during such a traumatic period of her life.

Sharing this unfortunate news with our mother in Rochester, New York, was especially difficult. She took the news rather sedately, internalizing her true feelings as she always did, believing as most mother's would that her son, Mark, would eventually contact her. I knew deep inside that he wouldn't and couldn't for reasons being.

Our remaining brothers and sisters not living in the

city were upset and in disbelief regarding this alarming news with the exception of Buddy, who was rather reserved; it was as if he felt or knew something we didn't.

Aunt Bessie was hysterical as she usually is in times of trauma and our older first cousins were extremely upset. Of course Aunt Bessie felt that Mark would soon contact her and I remember how my cousins Toni, Mario, and me tried to get her to understand that he couldn't. As usual, she cursed us out about a thousand times, reminding us that we were just children and didn't know what we were talking about. Yet, we sincerely felt and believed we did.

It now seemed as though whomever I was in the company of or wherever I went the general topic was the Bethune, Boyd, and Brown shootout with the Detroit STRESS Police Officers. The consensus amongst those in black communities was that these were some "BADD Brothers" who weren't jiving and that the dope houses better take cover. It was evident that those running the dope houses took this consensus rather seriously because doormen (armed guards) were walking off their posts declaring that the job was just too risky with the "3 Bee's (Bethune, Boyd, and Brown) on the prowl". Consequently, many drug houses out of blatant fear shut down their businesses. Those that were still in operation were heavily armed and were quite selective of who they did business with. I recall Mike being sick many days, waiting on someone to cop (purchase) his heroin for him because he wasn't welcomed in the local dope houses for obvious reasons; Mark Bethune was his brother! Talking about respect in the ghetto - if you were related to or an acquaintance of one of the "3 Bee's" it was automatic. However, this respect had somewhat of a strange aura. It was as though you possessed voodoo power or had the black plague. I began to feel as though I was a stranger in a foreign land, fearing no one, with the exception of the Police Department.

One morning, after having taken my daughter to school, I returned to my apartment and began thinking intensely about all that had happened regarding my brother, trying to put pieces together in an attempt to make some sense of all this. Abruptly, my thoughts were interrupted by a loud persistent banging on the door. My initial instinct was not to answer the door because I just wasn't in the mood for company, then I heard this soft male voice stating "Winnie, it's me. Open the door." I then replied, "Who is it?" And their reply was, "You know - Open the door." My reply to this was, "I do not recognize the voice; I'm not opening my door." Then there was this forceful baritone voice stating, "This is the goddamn police. Open the motherfucking door!" Petrified out of my mind, I nervously snatched the door open. All I saw from that point was a long barrel of a rifle pointed at my chest, with the voice demanding the whereabouts of my brother "Mark". Accompanying this huge plain clothes officer were 7 or 8 other plain clothes police officers in bullet proof vests. They searched the entire two bedroom apartment thoroughly including between the mattress and box springs and of course found no Mark, as I had attempted to tell them that he wasn't here and that I hadn't seen him since Thanksgiving. At this point I felt fear and rage and proceeded to tell them, "You're wasting your time; you'll never find Mark at any relative's home. He just simply would not jeopardize their safety and lives, especially the females." Then their reply was that I was being smart and I simply said "No, it's the truth." When I made a statement to the fact that they hadn't produced a search warrant, they stated that they didn't need one. Following that statement, they left as abrupt and disrespectful as they had entered. Shaking from head to toe I immediately concluded that I needed a stiff drink and proceeded non-stop to the liquor store. All I could think about as I briskly walked to the store was if I had sneezed the wrong way I could have been dead. Chuckling to myself, I thought how stupid those police officers were to even entertain the thought that my brother "Mark" who was as wise as an old owl, would hide out in an apartment of his youngest sister whom he cherished dearly, on the third floor with one way out. I now knew what I had already felt; that I was being watched from every angle by the Detroit Police Department and there was virtually nothing I could do about it.

That day my ex-husband and I concluded that it was just too risky, unsafe, not to mention psychologically unhealthy for Terri (our 6 year old daughter) to live at home in view of the circumstances. Therefore, she went to live with her father in Toledo, Ohio until this family trauma was resolved. It was indeed a relief to know that my daughter was now in a safe environment. As for myself, I felt like walking prey waiting on the next attack. Can you even imagine what kind of feeling that was - what my state of mind must have been like?

Family members were certainly not the only suspects targeted in the search for my brother, Boyd and Brown, who were now considered highly dangerous fugitives. All it took was a tip to the Detroit Police Department that the "3 Bee's" could be located at a specific place and off they were with artillery equipped for an army.

<u>The Detroit News - Wednesday, December 6, 1972</u> - **"Police Wrong in Two Raids" Woman Fear-Stricken as House is Searched**

It was 4:45 a.m. and Mrs. Caroline Tyler bolted awake to the frightening sound of loud and insistant knocking on her front door. At first she thought it might be her 18 year old daughter, Janet, and that she had forgotten the car keys to drive her father to work.

When she looked out the bedroom window and saw it was the police, she panicked, thinking that Janet had been in an accident. Rushing downstairs to answer the door, she came face-to face with another kind of terror. "The police had their guns drawn", said Mrs. Tyler, a 42 year old Social Worker for the Veteran's Administration Hospital in Allen Park. "They said they wanted to search my house. I just couldn't believe it. I was frightened nearly out of my mind." She said the police - in her fear she doesn't remember whether it was four or six officers - refused to tell her what they were searching for. "But I let them in," she declared. "I was wide-eyed with terror and I didn't think to ask them if they had a warrant. I just couldn't understand why they were standing in my house with drawn guns," said Mrs. Tyler, who is taking night graduate courses in social work from the

University of Michigan. "Here I have scrimped and saved with my family, been a good citizen and never been involved in trouble before, and there I was being searched like a criminal in my own home." She said the officers looked around her house, then demanded identification. When she produced it, they explained why they were searching the house. "They said that four policemen had been shot", she said. "Then they told me that they had the address of a suspect on this street, but when they got here, they found there was no such address. They said that because they couldn't find the address they had written down, they'd search the house with the next closest address, and that was my house." The officers left, she said, thanking her for her cooperation but not apologizing for the intrusion.

"I was absolutely frantic", she said. "You just have no idea what a frightening thing that is to go through. After they left and I pulled myself together I became angry. My God, is this City in a state of war? Must this City become a police state in order to survive?" Detroit Police District Inspector, James D. Bannon, who coordinated the raids and arrests after the shooting, said the search of Mrs. Tyler's house was 'technically" legal.

The Detroit News, December 6, 1972

Ann Arbor Co-eds are Routed in Nighties

State and Ann Arbor Police were red-faced today after smashing in the door of an Ann Arbor apartment and shooing several co-eds dressed only in nighties into the snow during a raid - on the wrong house. "They stomped in like gangbusters; we didn't know what was happening, so my roomate grabbed a baseball bat and the rest of us scrambled to get dressed", said Kathye Langstaff, one of five tenants in an Ann Arbor apartment four blocks from the University of Michigan campus. Armed with rifles and wearing bullet proof vests, Ann Arbor Officers entered the apartment at 10:45 p.m., Monday, shuffled the scantily clad girls onto a snow-covered porch, only to learn they were searching the wrong house. They had entered the two-story duplex on Packard but had arrest warrants for occupants of one of the units next door.

A later search of the correct apartment next door revealed that the suspects had moved out several months ago, state police said. "We got confused because of the way the units were numbered. Needless to say, we're extremely sorry", said Sgt. Ray Beamish of the State Police Ypsilanti Post. He said police units were acting on information supplied by Detroit Police in connection with the shooting early Monday of four Detroit Police Stress Officers in Detroit. "We had the right information, but the wrong house", he said. The girls accepted the apology but called the episode "traumatic". They said they are "hoppin mad" over the incident and may file suit under the 14th Amendment, which guarantees the right of privacy.

The Detroit News, December 11, 1972

Man Killed in Hunt for Shoot-Out Suspect

Detroit and Highland Park Police shot and killed a man early today in a suspected dope pad on Detroit's North side, where they were told they could find one of three fugitives charged with shooting and wounding four Detroit Policemen. Police identified the dead man as Darwood Foshee, 57, an apparent resident of the dwelling at 15744 Wabash, North of Puritan. Foshee was identified through fingerprints on file as the result of several past traffic warrants. He was dead on arrival at 2:45 a.m. at the receiving branch of Detroit General Hospital.

Highland Park Police said they received a tip that Mark Bethune, 22, was hiding at the Wabash address. They said Detroit Police were notified and several Detroit STRESS Officers accompanied them to the apartment. On arrival they said they were refused entry and that someone believed to be the dead man fired a shotgun through the front window. After returning the fire, police said they entered the apartment and found the man dead. They found no one else in the apartment, police said.

Since the December 4th Stress incident, it was standard procedures for inner city Detroit residents to be routinely questioned and harrassed for the mistaken identity of Mark, John B., and Hayward B., or some suspected connection with them. Heaven forbid if you weren't compliant; police brutality and even homicide was the end result. These incidents that I am referring to are the many that were never reported via the media.

Throughout the week I would converse with my family members in Rochester, New York and New York City and share with them the latest on Mark via conversing with others and through the media. We as Mark's family, eagerly relied on the media as did the general public for a daily update of the alledged incidents regarding Mark. We still had not heard from or seen him nor knew of his whereabouts. Quite frankly, deep within I felt that we wouldn't yet there was hope in my heart that we would. I was quite relieved that my mother was in New York and did not have to face the direct impact of this nightmare. I knew that this was her son and God only knows what she truly was experiencing.

The Federal Agents and the Rochester, New York Police Department were tactful, diplomatic and honest, admitting upon their initial visit to my mother's home that she and my brothers were under surveillance and naturally the phone was tapped. On another occassion the Rochester Police got a tip that Mark was at our mother's home and immediately surrounded it with police officers. With her permission they searched the house thoroughly and of course discovered that Mark was not there. She then explained to them that who her misinformed neighbors thought was Mark was her son Frankie, who was visiting from Ann Arbor, Michigan, yet had recently returned to Ann Arbor. The officers asked if she had a picture of Frankie and she showed them his graduation picture. They then asked if they could keep it for future reference and reluctantly she gave it to them with the officer assuring to return it. That very picture was not released from the Rochester Police Department until year 1993.

With knowledge that she was under surveillance 24 hours and now the Rochester, New York media reporting allegations about her son, my mother began experiencing much anxiety with many sleepless nights. She then began to spend more time at my sister Kitty and her husband's home where she felt more safe and comfortable. She also could be attentive to her new grandson which would relieve her mind of the intense situation with Mark.

Kitty, who at the time, was a teacher for the Rochester, New York School System, came home from work one day and saw that there were a couple of unmarked police cars in the driveway of her home. Our mother quietly opened the door and informed her that she had permitted the Federal Officers into her home because they wanted to speak to her about Mark. Kitty then greeted them, introducing herself as one of Mark's older sisters. They immediately asked her when was the last time she had seen her brother Mark. Kitty replied that the last time she had seen Mark was in 1968 when he came to Rochester for her stepfather's funeral. They then asked was Mark presently in her home and she replied, "no he wasn't". The officers then requested to search her home. Without hesitation she permitted them to. Kitty was so nervous and upset that she doesn't recall if they provided her with a search warrant. She further recalls them searching all 13 rooms of her double home extensively. "If your brother Mark should get in touch with you, we would like for you to tell him to surrender", they said. Kitty's reply to this request was that she didn't think she could tell him to do this, besides Mark was a strong willed person and she knew he wouldn't adhere to her request. Cautioned by the Federal Officers that she would be harboring a fugitive if she failed to do so; she assured them that she wouldn't put herself in the position of harboring a fugitive. She further stated that, "I don't feel my brother has done what you are accusing him of." Following that remark, Kitty thought about the last time she saw Mark in 1968 and how handsome, polite, caring and strong he had grown to be - and how firmly and securely he hugged her when he stepped off the Greyhound, as though he was the oldest instead of second to the youngest of her brothers.

The Detroit News, December 28, 1972

STRESS Officer is Slain

A Detroit STRESS Officer was killed and his partner critically wounded in a gun battle late yesterday. It occurred during a police stake out on a west side home for suspects in another STRESS shoot out December 4th. Dead of a head wound was Patrolman Robert Bradford, 25 year old father of three. His plain clothes partner, Patrolman Robert Dooley, 28, is in critical condition in Ford Hospital.

Shot in the chest, back and head, Dooley may be paralyzed permanently from the waist down if he survives, doctors said. From the hospital bed, Dooley managed to tell fellow officers he was sure the men who shot him and Bradford last night were John Percy Boyd, 23, formerly of 17154 Warrington, Detroit, and Hayward Brown, 18, of 12817 Strathmoor, Detroit.

Bradford and Dooley were shot at 5:45 p.m. yesterday in front of 9206 Schaefer, South of West Chicago, on Detroit's West Side. One of the two guns used in the shooting was also used in the December 4th incident, Police Commissioner John F. Nichols reported after ballistcs tests today.

District Inspector Gordon Smith, Co-comamnder of STRESS, said Bradford and Dooley were among four officers watching a house at 9259 Carlin on a "secret witness" tip that Boyd and Brown were inside. Carlin is the first street West of Schaefer and the shooting scene was to the rear of the staked out adrress. The city of Detroit had offerred rewards totaling $6,000 through the news "secret witness" program for information about Boyd, Brown, and Bethune. New contributions by the news last night increased the reward to $12,000. Police gave this version of yesterday's gunfight:

Bradford and Dooley were assigned with two other STRESS officers, Patrolman Charles Savage and Donald Lewis, to investigate "secret witness" tip in plain clothes and in two unmarked police cars. Savage and Lewis parked their car on Carlin to watch the front of the suspected house. Bradford and Dooley parked in a North - South alley East of Carlin and North of Westfield, in a location from which they could watch the rear of the house. Westfield, the first street South of West Chicago is the first street North of the suspected house.

About 5:40 p.m. two men left the house from the front, entered a car and drove away. Savage and Lewis notified Bradford and Dooley by radio that they would follow the two men. Dooley and Bradford then drove their car out of the alley, turned East on Westfield and then South on Schaefer, in case the two men who had left the front of the house were decoys and the suspects might leave by the rear. Bradford and

Dooley saw two men crossing Schaefer on foot near the middle of the block. The officers parked the car and approached the men. It is unclear whether the officers had an opportunity to identify themselves as police before being fired upon. One witness said the two men opened fire on the approaching officers apparently by surprise. Bradford fell to the ground immediately, and a witness said he was shot repeatedly after he fell. Dooley retreated to the police car, returning the gunfire as he moved back in an attempt to radio for help. The two suspects advanced on Dooley, shooting repeatedly, until Dooley fell in front of the police car from a bullet wound to the leg. The suspects stood over the fallen Dooley while one shot him three times as he lay in the street, according to an eyewitness. The suspect's attention was distracted at this point by a witness, Ronald Bryant, a private guard who left his nearby home when he heard the shooting and shouted at the gunmen. One of the men fired a shot at Bryant, who re-entered his house, where he watched from a window as the two men ran between houses on the east side of Schaefer.

Bryant later told police he had followed the men and saw them climb a six foot fence behind 9188 Schaefer, cross an alley to Hartwell, the next street to the east, and disappear between houses on the east side of Hartwell; meanwhile, Savage and Lewis had stopped the two men who had driven from the Carlin address, but found no reason to detain them and allowed them to proceed.

They then attempted to contact Bradford and Dooley by car radio and failing, returned to the area where they discovered the two had been shot. They called for help and dozens of police swarmed into the area, sealing it off to everybody but those who lived there, however, no further traces of the suspects was found.

Police said both of last night's gunmen are black.

Could the contents of what I had just read and viewed on a special news bulletin be considered factual? I thought - and how could this STRESS officer be sure that it was Boyd and Brown who had wounded him and killed his partner so late in the evening with darkness setting in? Besides, you know they say "we all look alike" anyway, as thoughts crept through my mind. Where was Mark? Why wasn't he again a suspect also? Well, not to my surprise as I continued to follow the news update regarding this incident, he miraculously became the primary suspect.

The Detroit News, January 1, 1973

Third Man Sought in STRESS Slaying

The addition of Bethune's name in the Bradford killing was announced yesterday by District Inspector James D. Bannon, Co-commander of STRESS, which stands for "Stop the Robberies, Enjoy Safe Streets". "Dooley was badly hurt, not too clear, and we were only able to talk to him briefly right after he was shot", Bannon said. "Therefore, we thought only two men were involved at first. Now that we have been able to talk to Dooley without the tubes in his mouth, Bannon said, we have a new name, Bethune, and Dooley says Bethune was the most aggressive of the three."

Dooley now states Bethune first opened fire, downing

Bradford and Dooley. He said Brown also fired shots but does not remember Boyd actually firing his gun, police said.

That which seemed so strange and odd to me the most was "why" were only four "STRESS" officers placed on a stake-out with prior knowledge that (2) alledged armed black gunmen "known" to shoot police officers on site may be occupying the dwelling that was being staked out? The intensity of this second STRESS incident had reached such magnitude that you could actually feel it in the air as I walked through the inner city streets of Detroit. Had the struggle reached the level of combative force by a mere 3 youthful militant black brothers or was these STRESS incidents merely coincidental?

Shortly after this incident, Detroit police officers entered the home of my sister Bunnie during mid-morning hours like gang busters. As her husband, still half asleep from having worked the midnight shift at the G.M. Cadillac Plant, attempted to tell the officers that he hadn't seen or heard from his brother-in-law, Mark; he was pinned to the sofa with the barrel of a rifle resting on his stomach by one of the officers, and told not to move. While pinned to the sofa the officers proceeded to search the house producing no search warrant. Upon leaving the house the officers took with them pages they had ripped from my sister's phone book, which consisted of all numbers in the A-B Section. The barrel of the rifle was lodged so heavily upon my brother-in-law's stomach, that it left a scratched circle imprint.

Bunnie was furious when she arrived home from work and discovered what had transpired in her home that terrifying day. The next day she went to the Detroit Police Complaint Department located in the Y.M.C.A. on Witheral and Adams. After submitting her complaint she was told that she would be contacted in a few days by investigative detectives. Some days later, two white detectives came to her home indicating that they were investigating the complaint she had made regarding the illegal search of her home, harrassment and police brutality of her husband while in search of her brother, Mark Bethune. They further stated that they would check records to find out which officers were on duty at the time and that those officers would be "advised" not to use that type of conduct in the future while visiting homes in pursuit of information. However, they left her with a message that was like a word to the wise. "Behind five officers having been wounded and now one dead, you're dealing with some trigger happy cops, who are naturally angry and frightened and it would be in the family's best interest to oblige as apposed to antagonize them." Bunnie did not reply because she felt that they were sympathizing with their fellow officers.

During this same week, Bunnie's brother-in-law came over to visit and upon leaving the house he was pushed up against his car by police officers and questioned about the whereabouts of Mark. When he insisted that he didn't know anything about his whereabouts the officers released him. This is when Bunnie knew that her family and home was under close surveillance.

Aunt Queen, who is our father's sister, called from her home in Chicago, Illinois that week to inform us that detectives had just left her home, questioning her about Mark's whereabouts. She simply shared with them that she had not seen her brother's youngest child since he was a baby. Then on another occasion, a close friend of Bunnie's, called her sharing that she had received the strangest call from a female stating that she was a friend of Mark's wanting to get in touch with him because she had a contribution to make to the "Cause". Her friend replied to the caller by stating that Mark was the brother of her friend "Bunnie" and that she personally did not know him. It was then concluded by Bunnie that Aunt Queen's number and her friend's number, whose last names began with the letter "B" were listed on the pages ripped from her phone book during the illegal search and misconduct at her home by Detroit police officers.

    The overall impact resulting from the great intensity of this now nationwide manhunt for our brother Mark and his alledged companions, made it seem as though we as his family members were just existing from one moment to the next. As for myself, I felt like a manual clock wound to its capacity, waiting desperately for even a minute of relief. The very thought of not knowing my brother's whereabouts and the overall status of his condition was truly exasperating. It was more than apparent that the Detroit Police Department felt we as family members, friends and the overall black communities knew something that could lead to Mark's, J. Boyd's and H. Brown's capture, because the harrassment, illegal searches and brutality was non-stop. They had now been labeled publicly by Detroit Police Commissioner John F.

Nichols as "Mad Dog Killers".

On January 11, 1972, Wayne County Circuit Judge Thomas J. Foley ordered police to refrain from harrassing relatives and friends of Mark, John Boyd, and Hayward Brown in view of numerous complaints and now misconduct charges that had been filed against the Detroit Police Department. He further threatened to incarcerate any police officers who did not abide by this order. Though this court order may have appeared to decrease the incidents of police misconduct, etc., it certainly did not stop it. This was evident throughout the black communities; with the manhunt continuing via normal operations.

The very next day, January 12, 1972, an incident occurred with the media reporting that the "exlusive trio" had surfaced again, now being accused of what was believed to be a bizarre fire bombing of the Planned Parenthood Office located in the Medical Plaza Building near Wayne State University. It was further reported that Hayward Brown was at the time carrying two loaded pistols and subsequently captured after a chase and struggle according to the police. Though it was alledged that Mark and John Boyd took part in this firebombing of primarily patient files and records, they were not captured. Ironically, on this very date, Bunnie was scheduled for her yearly check-up to renew her birth control pills via the "Planned Parenthood Birth Control Program". However, she had cancelled her appointment for some reason. I also received birth control pills at this very office. Instantly I thought about Mark's position regarding birth control devices being a form of genocide upon the black community and how he would lecture Bunnie and me about taking these dangerous and genocidal pills. Could this be another aspect of the mission in process?, I thought.

After a series of pre-trial examinations Hayward Brown was bound over for trial on charges of murder, assault and arson. After viewing the brutal beating that he had sustained during and after his arrest in an issue of the Jet Magazine, I questioned seriously if he would even make it to trial.

Various meetings were held with great numbers of Detroit residents attending regarding the police brutality and illegal tactics utilized in the manhunt for Mark, John B, and Hayward B. Also the Detroit City Council held a special hearing on charges of police brutality and harrassment in connection with the manhunt. I and other family members attended a rally in support of my brother Mark, Hayward B, and John B., in mid-January at Wayne State University to address illegal and unethical tactics being utilized in this intense manhunt and to renew previous demands that STRESS be abolished. This rally I shall always remember because I will never forget how my grandmother stood up amidst hundreds of people and shared how her grandson "Mark" had acquired his African identity "Ibo", how proud she was of him, the fear she felt for his safety, and the pain she felt not knowing where he was and how he was.

<u>The Michigan Chronicle</u>

<u>February 24, 1973</u>

"They Beat My Son to Death", says Mother of Suspect in Police

Officer Shooting

"I want to talk about it", Mrs. Katie Crew told the Chronicle as she sat, distraught and sobbing, in the office of Attorney Edward Bell. "I want to talk about it. They just beat my son to death." Mrs. Crew's son, Robert Slaughter, 29, reportedly shot Patrolman Gregory Ciaglo, from point-blank range when Ciaglo and his partner, Patrolman Maurice Harris, stopped Slaughter as he walked South on Second near Blaine, shortly after 2:00 a.m., February 9th. According to the police report, Ciaglo, who was driving, pulled up next to Slaughter to show him photos of the suspects in the December 4th and 28th STRESS shootings. Harris got out of the car and was walking around it when Slaughter drew a nickle-plated revolver and shot Ciaglo, the report says. Harris repeatedly fired several times at Slaughter at the rear of 831 Seward, where one policeman shot Slaughter in the leg when he "turned toward the officers with his gun in his hand". Patrolman Ciaglo was taken to Henry Ford Hospital, just 11 blocks away, where he was admitted, suffering "a no-exit gunshot wound to the jaw. His condition was listed as temporarily serious." However, Slaughter was taken to Detroit General, several miles farther away. Although suffering from what was later described by Attorney Bell as "a flesh wound to the leg", Slaughter was listed in "critical condition". In addition to the bullet wound, Slaughter was described as having incurred lacerations to the head. The police report explained: "As the officers attempted to handcuff the defendant, a violent struggle ensued and the defendant had to be forcibly subdued.

Mrs. Crew said she learned of her son's arrest when a friend called her. The friend told Mrs. Crew she "had heard" that Slaughter had been beaten. Slaughter had a record and had been recently released from prison. Mrs. Crew told the chronicle her response was, "if he has gotten in trouble with the police, I'm not even going down there". She said she did call the police and talked to "someone" who told her Slaughter "was in court". Last Tuesday, while she was at work, Mrs. Crew received a call from Detroit General. She was told that her son was in a coma. At the hospital, Mrs. Crew told the Chronicle, she learned that her son had been in a coma since he was admitted to the hospital. "His head was battered and swollen when I saw him", Mrs. Crew related, "I learned that he thrashed around a while after he got there (Detroit General), then lapsed into the coma. He never said anything or moved. Mrs. Crew talked with difficulty, fighting to keep her composure. "If he shot that policeman, he deserved to be arrested", she said. "That's what the law is for. But to beat him to death? They're not God or a judge. They had no right to just beat him to death. They shot him and captured him. There were no marks on his hands or arms. I believe they handcuffed him and beat him to death. He didn't have a chance", the distraught mother said, shaking her head.

"Our view, former Circuit Judge Bell told the Chronicle, as Mrs. Crew wiped her eyes, is that punishment is the exclusive domain of the courts - not the police. they have extracted from Robert Slaughter that which is higher than the maximum penalty in the state of Michigan. We are extremely upset about these incidents." Bell continued, "Even without pointing the accusatorial finger, it's almost as if a pattern is developing. It looks like we're sinking into a police state. Something has to be done." Asked what action he planned on behalf of his client, Mrs. Crew, Bell replied, "We intend to file a civil action...a law suit. this may not be the deterrant that's needed, but at this point, it's the only one available to us." "None of us are in favor of seeing a police officer or anyone else shot, Bell went on. We don't want the city overrun by law breakers - be they citizens or policemen. The courts are there to enforce the law without fear or favor. A policeman who breaks the law is no better than a Robert Slaughter who breaks the law. Nobody has the right to break the law - as we say was done in the case - and walk around without fear of prosecution. The sword has two edges". "They put in the newspapers and on t.v. when the policeman was shot, the former Circuit Judge pointed out, but there is only silence when this man was taken to the hospital in a coma and subsequently dies."

Slaughter's death was listed as a homocide on his death certificate. Cause of death - cranial cerebal injuries. His funeral was held Monday at the Cole Funeral Home on West Grand Blvd.

Following this brutal fatal beating of still yet another black male in the search for my brother Mark and John Boyd, the relentless manhunt resumes in full force, covering various cities throughout the country and Canada.

On February 24, 1973, a bulletin is flashed and the

media circulates that John Percy Boyd has been shot and killed late last night by Patrolman Bobby W. Davis in Atlanta, GA., who's suspicions were aroused by a man whom he thought was acting oddly. Patrolman Davis stated that after he tried to question this oddly acting man, a sawed off carbine came up from beneath his coat at which time he pointed it at Davis. Davis then stated he pushed the carbine aside and with his other hand, drew his revolver and shot and killed who was soon identified as John Percy Boyd. At this time, Patrolman Davis also heard other shots, turned and saw still another man with a pistol and thinking he was being fired upon returned the fire, shooting and killing this second man, who was soon identified as Owen Winfield, half-brother of John Boyd and a long time Atlanta resident. It was now highly suspected that Mark may also be in Atlanta and the Detroit Police Department announced that they were sending homicide detectives to Atlanta to determine whether Mark Bethune was hiding out there. There were also speculations and allegations that Mark may have been the "mystery shooter" responsible for firing two additional bullets found in Boyd's body, not fired by Patrolman Davis, and one additional bullet in Winfield's body, not fired by Patrolman Davis.

<u>Detroit Free Press - Wednesday, February 28, 1973</u>
HEADLINE - **STRESS Suspect Shot on Dorm Roof - Atlanta Officer Kills Mark Bethune**

Mark Clyde Bethune, a 22 year old Detroiter who helped spur the most extensive police manhunt in the city's recent history, was killed Tuesday afternoon by a single shot from the gun of an Atlanta Officer.

<u>The Detroit News</u> - Wednesday, February 28, 1973

HEADLINE - **Bethune Kills Himself in Atlanta - A Pledge of Death is Fulfilled**

The last of the suspects sought in the most intensive police search in recent Detroit history was killed yesterday. Ironically, while he was badly wounded by a shot from a policeman's .45 caliber gun, Mark Clyde Bethune, 22, died by his own hand. Bethune, shot in the chest and with police closing in on him, put his .357 magnum pistol to his head and pulled the trigger, ending his life.

The "hunt" is over. The final prey has been captured, and we as Mark's family thought the nightmare was over, yet through our lack of awareness, we failed to see that it had really just begun.

Awakening/Epilogue

My brother was referred to by most people as "Mark Clyde Bethune", those that sincerely knew him as Ibo and he bore many interesting labels from day 1 of the 86 day manhunt; gunman, mad dog killer, one of the 3 Bee's, insane-man, mastermind, mighty warrior, courageous one, one bad brother, mystery man, Jekyle/Hyde. We, as his family after having "finally" awakened from the startling nightmare of 21 years, today proudly refer to him and know him as Ibo Omar. It took the writing of this book, his life story, to bring about the awakening process to acknowledge and respect Ibo for who he truly was/is.

The old saying "sticks and stones may break my bones but names can never hurt me", just isn't quite accurate. Names can hurt you which has been quite evident throughout this book and so evident within this and all societies. We all possess the quest to know who we are, from where did we come, where we presently are, and to where are we going. All of these things that we are in search of have names/labels which can and will affect/effect our very existence. Kunte Kinte was willing to die for his name which was his heritage; Ibo Omar was also. How many of us are willing to give our life for our name, our heritage?

I often think about that day in January 1994 that I took on the responsibility of writing my brother's life story after having awakened that morning with the thought heavily on my mind, as though I had officially been given this task from some spiritual source. Jokingly, I say to myself that Ibo softly tapped me on the face several times in my sleep, telling me to wake up, that the time had come. Though I joke about this I am certain that it was he who assigned me this long overdue task. My daugher, Terri, a social activist by nature and heart, would often ask me, "When are you going to write Uncle Mark's life story; you've got the skills and the knowledge Ma", she'd say. I'd always reply, "Yes, I know. I'm going to do it." Well Terri G., I've done it! What do you think?

My mother, who lived with me at the time, was the first person I shared my intentions with and she was quite elated. "Are you really going to write the book", she kept asking me. I assured her that I was. She gave me the permission to write her son's life story and was the first person I interviewed. That interview and subsequent interviews took her back through some waters, she pledged never to tread again, which was very painful for her. Yet, without this vital history, this book would not have had it's foundation and for her input I am extremely grateful. Recently my mother sustained a mild stroke, which enhanced her pre-existing Parkinson's disease, leaving her with noticeable memory loss. She presently cannot recall Ibo's death and the events surrounding it, yet she does remember her son, which is truly a blessing. I became a bit stagnated behind this unfortuante event with my mother, yet my strong determination would not allow me to neglect my mission. I pray for but one thing as I write these very words; for my mother to witness the publishing of her son's life story - I am confident that the Almighty will make that possible.

Unveiling the past has not been easy. When you are discovering and re-living raw facts it becomes very difficult to digest. Compiling my brother's life story meant retracing "our" beginning, which consisted of many realities that I had neatly tucked away and did not want to remember and recent discoveries I am in the process of working through. Often while writing I would, without warning, break down from deeply within and cry profusely. At that point I would put down my pen, get in my car and take a tour of the city with Marvin Gaye's, "What's Going On", tape up loud enough for me to feel it through my soul. There is something about each song on that masterpiece that brings me so close to Ibo, especially his favorite, "Save The Children". Marvin's plea to save the children, save the little babies, is so astounding that it sends chills through your body. The message was so very clear - I cannot understand how we as African American people took this plea so mildly in the seventies and continue to do so to this very date. Ibo, my brother, spent endless days with his Save The Children Campaign, reaching out to the people to awaken them as to what tomorrow would bring if we didn't place our priorities on our children. I personally am ashamed of my negligence and ignorance for not having acted upon this most vital mission as soon as I should have. Instead, I was pretending to be a part of the solution when I in fact was very much part of the problem, fooling no one but myself.

Today I have dedicated my life to saving our children, to preserve our elderly and to maintain and restore African American families. This is what Ibo's mission was all about, pure and simple. Then why was there doubt as to who he was and what his purpose was? Well his mission was far beyond the realm of most imaginations to execute such a mission. Marvin's plea was not just to Ibo, John Boyd, Hayward Brown, and all those actively involved in The Movement, but to each and every African American adult who have innate invested interest in the salvation and preservation of their people. Yesterday, as I read an article in the December 1994 issue of the Ebony magazine about our fearless liberator/activist Harriet Tubman, I thought about the astounding courage it took to devise a plan utilizing an underground railroad to guide her people to freedom from enslavement. There was also a relentless manhunt for her with a reward for her capture in 1854 of $12,000, and all she did was develop a plan that proved beneficial in saving some of her people. This rekindled knowledge only re-enforces the unforgetable truth that black slavery was essential in the development of this country.

As I face my personal mission today, often I feel alone. "Where are the minds of my people? Why can't they see what I see?", I frequently ask myself. I now know what Ibo felt some 21 years ago - Where are the minds of my people? Why can't they see what I see? I see, as an African American woman, Director of a Community Drug and Education Prevention Program, mental health advocate, advocate of the elderly, recovering alcoholic/addict, mother, grandmother, aunt, great aunt, sister of "Ibo Omar", and a product of the inner city madness; the destruction of my people if they do not awaken, and I see no tomorrow as "Marvin" saw if that awakening does not take place soon and I mean "real" soon. It is now at this very moment, time for all African American adults who have made that transition to go to our villages which in America are our "communities" and save our children, preserve our elderly, our families, and our heritage with pride and dignity.

Daily I work with children and their families primarily African American on the Lower East Side of Detroit and other communities of the city that my mission may take me. Most of these children come from families that have simply given up and feel there is no hope for them in the year 1994 in the wealthiest and most prominent country of the world. The only solution readily available to them is alcohol, tobacco, crack/cocaine, heroin and other drugs, which they rely heavily upon.

In addition, the families of this community and similar communities are plagued with hunger/malnutrition, poor health, illiteracy, unemployment, extremely "high" - school drop out rates, without adquate clothing, no playgrounds - recreational/leisure activities to name a few "in the year 1994". This community and similar communities need more help than one could ever imagine. However, securing funds to continue our prevention community outreach effort has been quite difficult. As of the 1990 census, over 90 percent of this communities' population is of African American decent; I wonder if that's the problem? When I see and touch children in the year 1994 in Detroit's inner city hungry, dirty, with offensive body odors, with no socks, shoes with flapping soles or none, with no underwear, ragged and or one suit of clothing, I say again to African American adults who have made that transition: "Go to your villages (communities). Save your people."

We as the family members of Ibo Omar shall be forever indebted to him for his courageous efforts in the struggle of African American people. It is essentially important that we make known publically that we are in firm belief that Ibo Omar did not take his own life while on the dorm roof-top of Morris-Brown College in Atlanta, Georgia, February 27, 1973. Instead, we firmly believe that he was engaged in the activity of protecting his own life and while in so doing he became a victim of homocide. We have thoroughly examined Ibo's certificate of death and the autopsy report of the medical examiner and find the manner of death on the autopsy as being "undetermined". Then why was the media informed as they informed the public that Ibo committed suicide - naturally for obvious reasons. They wanted the public to believe that this deranged, mad dog killer, as he was so labeled, was so deranged that he took his own life. Yet it was evident on Ibo's Day that those he reached knew better.

The pleas of the seventies have become the crys of

today. So many youthful lives have been claimed via the drug wars and all they entail in the city of Detroit alone. A great percentage of African American male youth, ages 16-22, are incarcerated with sentences from 5 years to life. The psychiatric facilities have become revolving doors for youths unable to cope with day to day living, with children being admitted as early as the tender age of 5 years to these facilities. Family disintegration continues to grow with children being robbed of their foundations. Most important of all, children are being cut off from the necessary wisdom and guidance of the old folk.

Mothers that once weeped in privacy, cry out loud in desperation for help with their children - and the absence of fathers steadily increases. Now I ask what Marvin Gaye asked in 1971, "What's Going On" - Ibo persistently told me, yet I failed to listen. In 1993, while attending the African World Festival in Downtown Detroit, a young African male spoke to me and handed me a sheet of paper containing some striking knowledge that he and I discussed in great lengths. As we talked he handed this same information to each African American that walked by. This following information was on that sheet of paper - presented by T. Nelson, October 1992, "Stop the Maddness" - The Speech, By Willie Lynch, 1712 (Reprinted).

This speech was delivered to American slave and plantation owners in the eighteenth century. The speaker, Willie Lynch's name is best remembered in the user of the term "lynched", or more expressly put, the hanging of black slaves.

Ibo

Prior to Lynch's speech, hanging and other cruel forms of punishment were the norm for slave control. Then Lynch spoke this message in America. From that point on, slavery took on new dimensions. Once this plan was entrenched, it worked disatrously well. Use this knowledge to overcome the cruel impact of this plan, for the purpose to <u>UNITE</u> rather than to divide. "UNITED WE STAND, DIVIDED WE FALL":

Gentlemen:

    I greet you here on the bank of the James River in the year of our Lord one thousand seven hundred and twelve. First I shall thank you the Gentlemen of the Colony of Virginia for bringing me here. I am here to help you solve some of your problems with slaves. Your invitation reached me on my modest plantation in the West Indies where I have experimented with some of the newest and still the oldest methods for control of slaves. Ancient Rome would envy us if my program is implemented. As our boat sailed south on the James River, named for our illustrious King, whose version of the Bible we cherish, I saw enough to know that your problem is not unique. While Rome used cords of wood as crosses for standing human bodies along its old highway in great numbers, you are here using the tree and rope on occasion.

    I caught the whiff of a dead slave hanging from a tree a couple of miles back. You are not only losing valuable stock by hangings, you are having uprising, slaves are running away, your crops are sometimes left in the field too long for maximum profit, you suffer occasional fires, your animals are killed. Gentleman, you know what your problems are; I do not

Awakening/Epilogue 120

need to elaborate, I am not here to enumerate your problems, I am here to introduce you to a method of solving them.

In my bag here, I have a fool proof method of controlling your nigger slaves. I guarantee everyone of you that if installed correctly, it will control the slaves for at least 300 years. My methods are simple and members of your family or overseer can use it.

I have outlined a number of differences among the slaves; and I take these differences and make them bigger. I use fear, distrust, and envy for control purposes. These methods have worked on my modest plantation in the West Indies and it will work throughout the South. Take this simple little list of differences, think about them. On top of my list is "Age" but it is there only because it starts with an "a". The second is color or shade. There is intelligence, size, sex, size of plantation, status of plantation, attitude of owner, whether the slaves live in the valley, on a hill, east, west, north, south, have fine coarse hair, or is tall or short. Now that you have a list of differences, I shall give you an outline of action but before that I shall assure you that distrust is stronger than trust and envy is stronger than adulation, respect or admiration.

The nigger slave, after receiving this indoctrination shall carry on and will become self refueling and self generating for hundreds of years, maybe thousands.

Don't forget you must pitch the old nigger slave versus the young nigger slave, and the young nigger slave against the old nigger slave. You must use the light skin slaves versus the dark skin slaves and the dark skin slaves versus the the light skin slaves. You must also have your white servants and overseers distrust all niggers but it is necessary that your slaves trust and depend on us. They must love, respect, and trust only us.

Gentlemen, these kits are our keys to control, use them. Have your wives and children use them; never miss opportunity. My plan is guaranteed, and the good thing about this plan is that if used intensely for one year the slaves themselves will remain perpetually distrustful.

Thank you gentlemen.

End of Speech

by Willie Lynch

After having conversed at length with this young African American man, I was appalled by his knowledge, dedication and determination. The only concern that I have is that there are far to many singular African Americans trying to do the job of an entire "village" - as his last words were to me - "lack of unity is our downfall" - just as Ibo always said.

The wealth and abundance of knowledge that Ibo possessed in the late sixties and early seventies could have been passively stored and he could have chosen to pursue many alternative lifestyles then available; alcoholic/drug addict, drug dealer, hustler/pimp, flower child/hippie, vietnam suicide missionary, common laborer, bourgeoisie negro, etc. Now I ask this question of you who have taken the time to read his life story - which lifestyle would you have then chosen? My dear brother, Ibo, I ask this final question of you - "How accurate have I presented "your" life story?

                                                         Winnifred Bethune-Griffin